The Garden Room

The Garden Room

Bringing Nature Indoors

By Timothy Mawson

Photographs and illustrations by Ivan Terestchenko
Text by Alexandra Enders

Clarkson Potter/Publishers
New York

ACKNOWLEDGMENTS

My deep appreciation goes to the late Carlos Goez, my friend and partner at Pomander Bookshop in New York, who introduced me to America and to the world of books, for which I will always be grateful. My friends Ray Roberts and Bill Hamilton first proposed an idea for this book and offered significant help and encouragement throughout.

I must thank Ivan Terestchenko for his unique contribution, not only for his evocative photographs and charming watercolors, but for his spirit, enthusiasm, and friendship throughout this project. I am grateful to Alexandra Enders for her elegant text and ability to clarify my muddled thoughts with quiet understanding and professionalism.

Thanks go to Deborah Geltman, my agent, for her instinctive good sense and concern; Lauren Shakely, editorial director of Clarkson Potter, who had confidence in this book when it was just an idea; and my new editor, Annetta Hanna, for her guidance, encouragement, and support. Thanks to everyone at Clarkson Potter, especially art director Howard Klein and the designer of this book, Karen Grant.

I am honored by Horst P. Horst's generosity for the use of photographs from his private collection, and Rick Tardiff's assistance has been invaluable. A special "thank you" to Hitch Lyman and James Steinmeyer for original watercolors. I would also like to acknowledge Laboratoire Gorne of Paris for their support.

I am grateful to all the people who kindly allowed us to photograph their gardens, their rooms, and their various collections: Bill Blass, Jutta Buck, Nancy Cardozo, David Easton and James Steinmeyer, J. Barry Ferguson, Horst P. Horst, Robert Jackson, Ron Johnson and George Schoellkopf, Lee Link, Pamela W. Logan, Gregory Long, Hitch Lyman, Nancy McCabe, Phyllis Meshover and Michael Steiner, Renny Reynolds, Tommy Simpson and Missy Stevens, Jessica Tcherepnine, Michael Trapp, Bunny Williams, and Peter Wooster.

Thanks also to my good friends Barbara Leaming and David Parker, for always lending sound advice and good humor; Tina Dodge, whose talent, inspiration, and love have made everything bloom; Deborah Webster, for her good judgment and helpful advice; Chris Zaima, for many kindnesses; and Jane Fredrikson, who looked after the shop during numerous absences.

I am grateful, finally, to my most important collaborator, Gael Hammer, whose intelligence, taste, and spirit inform every page.

Printed in Singapore

Library of Congress Cataloging-in-Publication Data
Mawson, Timothy
   The Garden Room / by Timothy Mawson; photographs and
   illustrations by Ivan Terestchenko; text by Alexandra Enders.
      Includes index.
      1. Garden rooms—U.S.   2. Interior decoration—U.S.
   —History—20th century.   I. Terestchenko, Ivan.
   II. Title
   NK2117.G37M38   1994
   728'.9—dc20   93-19680

   ISBN 0-609-80282-8

   10 9 8 7 6 5 4 3 2 1

   First Paperback Edition

CONTENTS

Introduction

As one more inclined to green thoughts than to green thumbs, for me the words *garden room* have always had a mellifluous air, a suggestion of shelter and ease. They also conjure up very pleasant memories. As a young man I frequently spent school holidays with an aunt and uncle at Field House, their eighteenth-century stone house near Giggleswick in the Yorkshire Pennines. The garden room was situated in a recent addition to the main building, constructed, by a bizarre coincidence, from some of the thick stones of the demolished nursing home where I had been born sixteen years earlier. The room was immensely comfortable, furnished with chintz-cushioned rattan garden furniture, popular in the 1950s, and scattered with books, newspapers, and magazines. A collection of family photographs stood on a desk in one corner of the room, and I remember the romantic watercolors of John Sell Cotman on the walls. A fireplace faced low windows across the room that looked out over the countryside. French doors led to a rose garden, and a rectangular lawn lay beyond with herbaceous borders on three sides enclosed by an old stone wall.

From March through September the garden room was in constant use by family and dogs—newspapers read in the morning, a drink before lunch, and, if possible, forty winks afterward, falling asleep to the sound of the birds outside. Here my uncle, dressed in hunting pink, ate a boiled egg after every meet, and tea was served to the rest of the family. Here my aunt arranged flowers, wrote letters, and painted watercolors in the afternoon. The garden was always right there, beautiful and inviting. If we weren't too deep in our armchairs, we would get up and stroll around, deadhead a few roses, and then go back for another look through *Country Life*. To me, a garden room is all about this kind of casual charm.

In its most basic incarnation, a garden room is simply a place in which to enjoy the garden, whether it's an indoor room looking out, a transition area between house and garden such as a porch or terrace, or a freestanding structure within the garden itself. Garden rooms are unique in that they tend not to have a specific function, though they can be used for any number of activities. Designed primarily for pleasure, these spaces combine the arts of interior decorating and gardening. Unlike living rooms (public) or kitchens (functional), they present an opportunity to experiment with color and texture, to create moods, and to explore attitudes about nature in a setting that is both private and whimsical. Some are rustic, seemingly untouched by the human hand; others are highly civilized. In writing this book, I thought we needed to take a closer look at this often-neglected area.

7th July

My interest in garden rooms is closely tied to my own evolution in life as a bookseller. In the 1970s I was a partner at Pomander Bookshop in New York, which specialized in general antiquarian books. At the time I believe we offered only two titles dealing remotely with gardening, Francis Bacon's famous essay *Of Gardens*, which begins "God Almighty first planted a garden; and, indeed, it is the purest of human pleasures," and Sir George Sitwell's *On the Making of Gardens*—and even those we had more for their literary than horticultural associations. My life changed when a friend gave me a list of old gardening books he was looking for. Little did I know that my hunt for these authors would draw me more and more into the extraordi-

GERTRUDE JEKYLL
A Vision of Garden and Wood

nary world of gardens and flowers on which so much has been written and illustrated for almost five centuries. "We have no other literature," observed H. E. Bates, "in which grace and information, charm and science, have gone on for so long together." You could say that my love of gardens and gardening began then, though I should confess that I'm not a true gardener, in the sense that I'd rather be arranging flowers or directing from an armchair than grubbing in the soil.

My friend's list included mainly late-nineteenth- and early-twentieth-century English garden writers such as William Robinson, Gertrude Jekyll, Eleanor Sinclair Rohde, Shirley Hibbard, and E. A. Bowles. Most of these names are familiar now, but twenty years ago they had all but been forgotten. Searching for books by these writers quickly became an obsession; although earlier works such as herbals and the richly illustrated eighteenth- and early-nineteenth-century botanicals were already quite scarce, at the beginning it was still possible to find a wide range of books. Demands for information on garden history, landscape design, monographs of flowers and shrubs, plant hunting, herbs, botanical illustration, and flower painting and decoration poured in as I became known for carrying these subjects.

PREVIOUS PAGE: *A rocking chair enveloped in a bower of climbing vines, topiaries, and potted plants on the front porch is a favorite place to rest in the afternoon.* OPPOSITE, TOP: *A watercolor shows the back of our 1700s house and the attached deck off the garden room.* CENTER: *My library contains books on all aspects of flowers and gardening, including flower-painting instructions with exquisite hand-colored illustrations.* BOTTOM LEFT: *A handwritten letter from Gertrude Jekyll, found in a book, gives directions to Munstead Wood, her home in Sussex.* BOTTOM RIGHT: *An illustration from Thomas G. Gentry's* Nests, Eggs and Birds of the United States, *1882, depicts a barn swallow.* THIS PAGE, TOP: *The garden room, once an ice house, opens onto a white garden, fragrant and radiant in the summer. Millie the pug relaxes next to a nineteenth-century Copeland and Garrett porcelain seat in the shade of flowers and herbs.* LEFT: *A watercolor sketch shows me lost in a book.*

Regular trips to England proved fruitful, and the search, often in obscure places, was never dull. What excitement to find a vellum edition of William Robinson's *The Wild Garden;* a signed copy of Vita Sackville-West's poem "Sissinghurst," published by the Hogarth Press; or the early editions, in their friendly buckram bindings, of Gertrude Jekyll. (And there were other benefits as well—once, digging through a box of books in a chilly barn, I came across a letter written from Munstead Wood in Miss Jekyll's own hand.) Who could resist Jason Hill's *The Contemplative Gardener,* Sacheverell Sitwell's *Old Fashioned Flowers,* or the amusing novels of Beverley Nichols detailing the joys and misfortunes of his garden? I began unearthing books by American writers, too—Louise Beebe Wilder, Mrs. Francis King, Alice Morse Earle, and Celia Thaxter's *An Island Garden* with its wonderful illustrations by Childe Hassam —and discovered that there was equally as much passion and knowledge on this continent.

When I moved to Connecticut in 1984 and opened a gardening-book shop in a restored 1800s mill—turned—country store in the village of New Preston, I knew that I wanted to create not just a store but a garden room of sorts. Painted bookcases hold the bulk of my stock, but all the gardening odds and ends I've accumulated—terra-cotta pots, old tools, wood finials, cast-iron urns, and a selection of garden benches—are spread through-

TOP: *Ivan sketched this amusing heading for a* carnet de voyage, *illustrating our experiences working on this book.* CENTER: *A collage displays some of the ephemera on flowers I have collected over the years from seed packets and catalogs.* RIGHT: *Hidden in a Victorian scrapbook of flowers, a family of mice is discovered when the string is pulled.* OPPOSITE, TOP: *We created this tableau in homage to Vita Sackville-West, perhaps the most influential gardener of our time.* CENTER: *My collection of miniature garden tools in wood is set against a painting of a French* jardinier.

out. In the center of the room a wide table holds extra books, prints, topiaries, old seed catalogs, and whatever other objects I've been able to obtain recently. Architectural and botanical prints, lithographs, and engravings fill an old yellow wheelbarrow. French doors open out onto a deck overlooking the river and a cottage-style garden nestled in the foundation of another old mill beyond. In the summer, under the direction of my friend Tina Dodge, window boxes on either side of the entrance are planted with masses of old-fashioned 'Azure Pearls' petunias, lavender, teucrium, oxypetalum, convolvulus, and *Artemisia stellarana*. Containers overflow with lemon, lime, and a variety of mint geraniums, nicotiana 'Sissinghurst', yellow sage, and parsley. A five-year-old fig tree planted in a weathered barrel shares its space with purple fennel and sage, red verbena, 'Summer Madness' petunias, and ivy. With the sound of rushing water, the scent and vibrant color of the plants combine to create a magical effect, enhancing the very literary garden that grows within.

Garden rooms are nebulous things. There have always been structures in the gar-

den, of course, from the simplest arbors intended for a moment's rest to intricately carved open-air marble palaces for sleeping in hot climates. The ancient Egyptians, Babylonians, and Indians all built summerhouses and shady pavilions as part of their gardens. Colorful tents with canopies and curtains were set up for feasting and relaxing—the Old Testament's Book of Esther describes the Persian king Ahasuerus's luxurious pleasure pavilion "where were white, green, and blue hangings, fastened with cords of fine linen and purple to silver rings and pillars of marble: the beds were of gold and silver, upon a pavement of red, and blue, and white, and black marble" (1:6). Roman estates had nymphaeums (small temple-like marble buildings fitted out with water) for dining, and Pliny the Younger recounts that in his garden was found "a chamber of lustrous marble, whose doors project and open upon a lawn." At her summer villa in Prima Porta, Augustus Caesar's wife Livia commissioned an underground room (which, as Pliny says, "in the midst of summer retained its pent-up coolness") to be painted in continuous garden murals and trompe l'oeil, with colorful birds, flowers, trees, and shrubs. The Romans also created grottoes—including some built into the cavities of enormous tree trunks—that served as dining rooms, as well as dining platforms fashioned into the boughs of large trees, a tradition that was adopted again during the Renaissance. A seventeenth-century engraving shows a famous tree house at Pratolino, a dining platform in a massive oak tree reached by two semicircular staircases with rustic handrails carved out of the trunk. In Elizabethan England, revelers frequently erected pavilions for special banquets. In the 1629 *Paradisus*, John Parkinson advised planting "the Jacimine, white and yellow, the double Honeysocke, the Ladies' Bower, both white and red and purple, single and double . . . to set by arbors and banqueting houses that are open before and above, to help to cover them, and to give both sight, smell and delight." What these rooms have in common is that they were all built for enjoyment, for the tangible satisfaction of the senses and ease of the spirit.

More permanent garden structures and summerhouses, small buildings constructed both for architectural interest and for practical use, were made of brick and stone. A good description of one comes from John Rea in his 1665 *Flora, Ceres and Pomona:* "a handsome octangular somer-house roofed everyway and finely painted with Landskips and other conceits furnished with seats about and a table in the middle which serveth not only for delight and entertainment but for many other necessary purposes, as to put the roots of tulips and flowers in, as they are taken up upon papers, with the names upon them untill they be dried, that they may be wrapped up and put in boxes." Occasionally summerhouses, sometimes called, evocatively, shadow houses, were open on all sides, with delicate columns supporting the roof. John Worlidge, author of *Systema Agriculturae, Vinetuem Britannicam,* and *Systema Horticulturae,* hit upon one of the pleasant secrets of garden houses; in 1669 he wrote that "the more remote it is from your house, the more private you will be from the frequent disturbances of your Family or Acquaintance." By the eighteenth century, in England at least, the

passion for landscaping had produced magnificent estates littered with temples, grottoes, Gothic ruins, pagodas, and other "eye catchers," as William Kent called them.

To some people a garden room means strictly a greenhouse, conservatory, or solarium. Although there's evidence that the ancient Romans built hothouses with windows made of thin talc or mica for raising tender specimens, the first glass conservatories appeared in Europe in the seventeenth century. Meant to conserve delicate vegetation brought from more temperate climes, these elaborate, formal structures were sometimes used as winter gardens. Noblemen built orangeries, filled with tubs of the precious citrus tree, and gave parties where guests could pick their own fruit. (In 1666, Samuel Pepys records seeing oranges growing in Lord Brooke's garden at Hackney: "I pulled off a little one by stealth [the man being mightily curious of them] and ate it, and it was just as other little green small oranges are—as big as half the end of my little

ABOVE LEFT: *A turn-of-the-century cold frame placed in a corner of the kitchen garden now stores tools, pots, cloches, and plants.* ABOVE RIGHT: *This nearly life-size wooden trade sign, designed to sell hoses, keeps me company in the garden.* OPPOSITE, TOP: *The boxes in front of my shop in New Preston are planted each year by my friend Tina Dodge; they overflow with 'Azure Pearls' petunias, browallia, nierembergia, sage, artemisia, and cascading ivy.* BOTTOM: *Passionflowers frame the windows on either side of the shop's entrance in summer.* FAR RIGHT: *Ivan sketched me relaxing on location.*

finger.") Advancing technology, the availability of materials such as cast iron, and the interest in exotic plants were responsible for the proliferation of greenhouses in the Victorian era. The seventy-foot-high Palm House, built in the 1840s at the Royal Botanical Gardens at Kew to fit tropical trees, inspired that most famous glass house, Joseph Paxton's Crystal Palace, which he designed for the Great Exhibition of 1851. On a more modest scale, Wardian cases, originally built for traveling plants, and glassed-in extensions of the main house became possible, bringing the garden into the drawing room.

In America there have always been garden rooms, though we don't tend to know them by that name. The vagaries of the climate and the vernacular aesthetic have produced unique architectural and horticultural expressions—screened or glassed-in porches, gazebos, and sun rooms are just a few of the forms garden rooms have taken. There are grand American historical examples certainly, such

as Mrs. Phipp's garden room at Old Westbury Gardens on Long Island; the arched Gothic conservatory at the private estate called Rockwood, built in 1852 near Wilmington, Delaware; and the two garden houses at Mount Vernon, George Washington's home on the Potomac in Virginia. But, more important, there is a living tradition, people creating rooms with the glow of the garden about them for entertaining, dining, relaxing—and, of course, for actual gardening.

I have dwelt on very grand examples, but there were and are plenty of more idiosyncratic and eccentric garden rooms, especially among those made today. Increasingly, garden rooms have come to be seen as a pleasant necessity. My own garden room is a case in point. My partner, Gael Hammer, and I settled in an eighteenth-century miller's cottage in Washington, Connecticut, just a few minutes from the shop. Attached to the main building off the kitchen was an abandoned icehouse that we turned into a comfortable study

and garden room. On the cathedral ceiling artist Carol Anthony painted five plump pears over puffy clouds and a blue sky. The pears represent the inhabitants of the house, including two royal poodles, Rupert and Oliver, with the smallest pear, napping over an oval window, depicting Guinness the cat. Much of the time we use the garden room as a study and a spring dining room, where we are in close

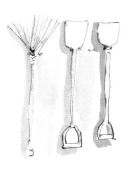

proximity to the garden and the fragrance of the flowers. A long trestle table holds books, antiques, and the miniature garden tools, furniture, and pots I've collected for several years. One of my most prized possessions is an extremely rare lead flower garden, made in England by F. Britain in 1924 as a child's toy. This, I might add, is the ideal garden to have. No watering, no maintenance. During the winter

months, many of the flowering plants and topiaries from the terrace and porch take up residence here.

To the left and right are French doors. One set leads to a courtyard and Moon Garden, where at night the white flowers glow in the moonlight and the fragrant *Nicotiana alata* 'Grandiflora' and 'Casablanca' lilies hold court with the datura and heliotrope. On the opposite side, doors open onto a deck covered with terra-cotta pots filled with eucalyptus, plumbago, tibouchina, petunias, and nierembergia,

TOP LEFT: *Tiny tools fascinate me and make wonderful props, such as these wooden ones placed among myrtle topiaries and a cut-out cardboard figure.* TOP RIGHT: *This eighteenth-century Staffordshire porcelain gardener clutches a spade and a pineapple.* RIGHT: *An ordinary tomato gives scale to a tiny urn in this model greenhouse, shown with thimble-sized terra-cotta pots and a metal watering can.* OPPOSITE, TOP LEFT: *Red hibiscus flowers make an exotic headdress for this unusual pitcher.* TOP RIGHT: *A model wooden plow offsets a seventeenth-century Diderot print of agricultural implements.* CENTER: *The garden room's cathedral ceiling was painted by Carol Anthony.* BOTTOM: *Rupert and Oliver are our two royal poodles.*

all of which make up a palette of pink, purple, mauve, silver, and blue. A Chinese Chippendale–style railing entwined with 'Heavenly Blue' morning glories, 'Violet Glow' asarina, and purple passionflowers (*Passiflora × alatocaerulea*) encloses the deck. In summer we dine here by candlelight, surrounded by a bower of flowers, scented herbs, and the twinkling of fireflies.

We wanted to create living spaces around the house, and besides the Moon Garden and deck off the garden room there is a kitchen courtyard, enclosed by a wrought-iron fence where hummingbirds flit to and fro rifling all the blossoms, and a wide porch that wraps around the south side to the front of the house. These outdoor rooms and spaces are all different, fairly small, and intimate; each is quite separate from the others and is designed to be used at different times of the day. We wanted the garden to evoke particular moods and still convey a sense of symmetry and unity as a whole. Fragrance and color were extremely important, and the same color schemes repeat throughout the beds, with different plant material in each area. As William Beach Thomas noted, "A garden may be said to be the aura of a home. Without it a country house or cottage lacks its right and proper atmosphere, and is left as bald as a small child's drawing."

There's nothing magnificent about my garden room or, for that matter, any of the

twenty rooms pictured here. Instead of being displays of grandeur, these quirky spaces are expressions of temperament and taste. They are the work of individuals, creative people, not only professional gardeners but designers, decorators, artists, and writers, whose love of the garden has prompted them to interpret the garden room after their own interests and passions. If gardens are personal, garden rooms are equally so, and they're often extensions of their creator's personality. In organizing this material, I felt strongly that there was a group of garden rooms distinctly country in feeling, some rustic, some old-fashioned, and some quite literally used for gardening activities. Other rooms act as studios or places to bask in the love of garden things—such pleasures as books, antiques, and botanical paintings. Still others, often separate buildings in the garden, are more fanciful, allowing the owners to create fantasy in the form of a temple for solitary musing or a greenhouse for showcasing sculpture.

Though all the people shown here have gardens, I think that the love of the garden, and things of the garden, transcends the need for actual flower beds or vegetable patches; I could well imagine a garden room devoted to flowers or botanical books in the grayest of cities. As we photographed the book, we asked each host what he or she valued most. "Time" and "privacy" were the two luxuries that came up over and over again. The very different garden rooms in our final section capture these desires, and it seems to me that in our quest for these elusive qualities lies the answer to why we make garden rooms.

ABOVE: *The covers on E. A. Bowles's* My Garden in Summer *and* My Garden in Autumn and Winter *were decorated by Katherine Cameron.* TOP RIGHT: *This early Staffordshire figure looks quite awed by his green thumb.* OPPOSITE: *My desk in the garden room is always cluttered with books, prints, and objects. The ceiling shows a pear for each inhabitant of the house, including our two poodles and Guinness, the cat.*

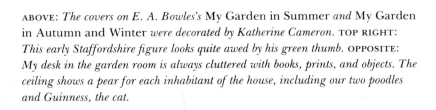

Country Garden Rooms

Rustic Refinement

Like any place that has known great happiness, a slight nostalgia pervades the stone house in Connecticut's Litchfield Hills, where Nancy Cardozo lived with her husband, Russell Cowles, until his death in 1978. For twenty-five years they lived and worked in creative harmony, she writing, he painting. They reconvened from separate studios for quiet lunches—talk was reserved for dinner—and walks down to the stream or up the nearby hill to pick blueberries. "We ate in the shade of the arbor and danced under the starry skylight of the studio," Nancy wrote in *Creature to Creature,* a collaborative work of poems and sketches. Though Russell died many years ago, the house today still suggests his presence—his crisp landscape paintings decorate the walls, and his photograph adorns the bedroom. Wistfulness flickers and vanishes as Nancy speaks of the past, and the atmosphere of the property, depending on the clouds overhead and the wafting of warm breezes, ranges from melancholic to romantic to euphoric, like the restored stone silo, open to the sky: on gray days it towers to the heavens like a medieval ruin; on sunny days it's a fairy-tale leaf-strewn changing area for the nearby pool.

The house itself is stucco-covered stone, built in the 1820s by an affluent Englishman, no doubt in the manor style of his home county, with two pointed Gothic windows high on either side. The front facade is blunt and classical, with two rows of evenly spaced ordinary windows and a paved path leading directly to the door. (In 1839 the house—including 100 acres—sold for $250.) When Russell bought the place in 1940, he made few changes to the exterior; he patched up

holes and added a lintel, a pineapple flanked on either side by two round balls, made of carved wood covered in stucco.

Off the back of the house sits what had been the original owner's manger for livestock, with an enclosed hayloft above. Exposed on one side, with two doors on the facing wall, the lower space feels both sheltered and airy, the darkness lit up by sunlight on the green fields beyond. Russell and Nancy paved the earth floor and installed a grill for cooking, but the feel of the place, with its stone walls and coarse timber ceiling, is still marvelously primitive, even a bit brutish. With smoke, snow, and "an imported shaggy pony," Nancy's son, Jan Egleson, a film director, turned it into a sixteenth-century Irish manor hall for a television series several years ago. Stacked logs line one wall, and huge stone slabs step up into the main house. As boys, Nancy's sons slept in the large whitewashed loft above the garden room, and the whole family still gathers here for meals and to celebrate birthdays, anniversaries, and other happy occasions. A thirty-year-old trumpet vine frames the view toward the stream and hill, and the fragrance of alyssum and twining roses drifting from Nancy's gray-green garden sweetly suggests the summer nights when, as Nancy wrote, "eating by candlelight, in the breezeway that once housed sheep and cows, we talked the hours away."

PREVIOUS PAGE: *Nancy Cardozo, photographed by her son Nick Egleson.* OPPOSITE: *Flowers fill a blue enamel pitcher in a doorway of the garden room.* TOP: *Russell Cowles designed the pineapple lintel above the door of the stone house.* CENTER: *The house dates from the 1820s.* BOTTOM: *Russell's oil painting of the house captures its mood.* FOLLOWING PAGE: *Called the "breezeway" by the family, the garden room is cool and inviting on hot summer afternoons.*

OPPOSITE: *A watercolor portrait of Nancy by Ivan depicts her enjoying a quiet moment in the garden room.* TOP LEFT: *The garden room leads to the house via a set of New York State granite slabs.* BOTTOM LEFT: *A photo by Ernest Knee shows the stone house as it appeared when Russell Cowles bought it in 1940. Once a manger for cattle and sheep, the garden room is now home to more fanciful animals, such as a fresco cow, painted by Russell on plaster and wood,* TOP RIGHT, *and a rusty owl lantern,* BOTTOM RIGHT.

Elements of
Porch Hospitality

Few people who have read Louise Beebe Wilder, an early-twentieth-century garden writer and devoted plantswoman, can avoid falling under her spell. Her lyrical, informative, and inspiring books—she wrote ten from 1916 until the time of her death in 1938, as well as scores of gardening articles—are as germane today as when they were first published. Most haunting are the evocations of her own beloved garden, Balderbrae, in Pomona, New York, which she and her husband, an architect, created together, using his plans and her plantings. When interior designer and architect David Easton and his partner, artist James Steinmeyer, bought the property from the Wilders' daughter in 1980, all that was left of Louise's magnificent garden were some of the retaining walls and huge cement pots that Walter Wilder had made for his wife, the barest outlines of the plantings, and the small house where she wrote her books. (With its stone walls, French doors, and latticework, this cottage, now a guest house, influenced the style of the building that Easton eventually constructed across the garden.) "Even with crumbling walls and rampaging weeds it was a magical place," says David, and he and James called in Nancy Goslee Power, a garden designer who was familiar with Louise's work, to renovate the grounds. Today the garden, though far simpler and shadier than formerly, is both subtle and lush, with pale soothing hues and harmonies, and soft tints of purple and gray among the greens.

David Easton's trademark as a designer is an elegant hospitality. He believes in simple, all-purpose rooms, and so the largest section of his house is a "hall" for sitting, visiting, and eating next to the fireplace, in the manner of an

old French château. And he almost always makes porches part of the houses he designs. (He has said of kindred spirit Bunny Williams: "Bunny is someone who understands a screened porch. There aren't many of those people left.") All in all, then, it is not surprising that when he built a house for himself, he added two very substantial porches to his basic rectangle, with part of the garden framed between the porches and the rest extending beyond. Each porch is covered above and on three sides, with the front staggered with open trellis work; each also has a porthole at one end, setting off a particular view of the garden. The porches are not screened because, as James says, "it never gets as buggy here as one imagines it will."

As far as porches go, these are so well furnished that they're really much more like open-air rooms than sheltered spots in the garden. In design the two porches are very similar, with the same white walls and stone floors giving onto a gravel courtyard. They strike different moods, however. The sitting porch is extremely snug, littered with books, vases, carved wooden objects, birdcages, and a whole collection of small chairs, ranging in size from a few inches to knee high. The focal point is a great, dark fireplace, inspired by a visit to an old hotel in Maine's Northeast Harbor. The set of rattan chairs and matching sofa, appointed with crisp red-and-white-striped pillows, belonged to David's parents.

Whereas the sitting porch has a friendly, cluttered air, the dining porch is sparser and more dramatic. White chairs and benches repeat the lattice motif, while heavy black tools hang from the wall, more for display than for use, though the rake occasionally gets taken down for a run through the gravel. But from either porch it's possible to sit and enjoy the garden, mulling over Louise Beebe Wilder's words in *Color in My Garden*: "Each within his green enclosure is a creator, and no two shall reach the same conclusion; nor shall we, anymore than other creative workers, be ever wholly satisfied with our accomplishment. Ever a season ahead of us floats the vision of perfection and herein lies its charm."

PREVIOUS PAGE: *The wisteria-laden loggias are cool and tranquil.* OPPOSITE: *Color and texture play a crucial role in the details of each room, such as the placement of this quirky wooden fruit near a sculptural hosta leaf.* ABOVE: *A porthole window, above a grouping of myrtle and eugenia topiaries, looks down the length of the loggia.*

TOP LEFT: *A bird's-eye view of the house and gardens was painted by James Steinmeyer.* TOP RIGHT: *This nineteenth-century print of a woodman is displayed on the sitting porch.* BOTTOM LEFT: *The guest house, shown beyond a large armillary sphere, was once Louise Beebe Wilder's writing room.* BOTTOM RIGHT: *An iceberg rose graces a 1930s metal vase.*

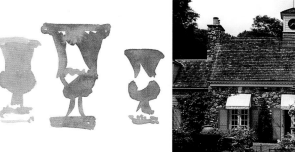

TOP: *The snug sitting porch is full of books, vases, and favorite wooden objects; its focal point is a great dark fireplace.* CENTER: *The house reveals a graceful symmetry.* RIGHT: *David Easton.* FOLLOWING PAGE: *The garden, planted with lamb's-ears, lady's mantle, geranium 'Johnson's blue', sedum, and petunias, frames the sitting porch. Geraniums, vinca, and alyssum fill Walter Wilder's cement pots. Isle Icron Superior roses climb onto the innovatively trellised porch roof.*

TOP LEFT: *Mapp, a Norfolk terrier, relaxes in the sun.* TOP RIGHT: *Elements such as rattan furniture, a big fireplace, and hanging lanterns make the sitting porch, shown here in a watercolor by James Steinmeyer, very comfortable.* ABOVE LEFT: *In June, Isle Icron Superior roses climb the trellis to festoon the porches.* ABOVE RIGHT: *A shady border near the loggia, made with columns designed by Mr. Wilder, contains sea foam roses, foxgloves, hostas, and petunias.* OPPOSITE, RIGHT: *Coffee is taken in the garden room.* BOTTOM: *James Steinmeyer.*

A Place to Rest

and Remember

In a Washington, Connecticut, garden laid out with pleasing logic, there were still plenty of twists and turns, hidden views, and unsuspected vistas. The corner where the brick retaining wall met the hedge was not, however, one of the successful aspects of this landscape. Owners Ron Johnson and George Schoellkopf called it "the Bermuda triangle," because the space was so resolutely lost. The solution eluded them until they realized, after several years of strenuous work, that there was no place to rest in the garden. Their small garden house, recently finished, became the "necessary completion." The attention to detail that makes their garden a joy of ordered spontaneity, from the triangular clipping of box hedges to the romping of spring violets up and down the widely set granite steps, is evident in the building's carefully placed double French doors and the gable pitched to match the addition on their 1760s saltbox house.

The light-filled, airy interior, usually furnished with a sturdy table, alternates as dining, resting, and work space. In summer, dinner by candlelight is a feast for the senses, awash in the fragrance of the climbing roses and the rustlings of the garden. On a hot afternoon the house is cool and shaded, offering a refreshing view of the stream. The decoration is minimal and idiosyncratic. A dresser along one wall holds a collection of blue and white bowls, ceramic pots, and other odds and ends that have made their way down from the main house. Though George acknowledges that he tends to "overplant everything," he finds the now-bare exterior a tad severe and plans to espalier it with evergreen holly.

It's impossible to speak of this garden room without mentioning the overall

garden, each part of which was painstakingly conceived and executed. From the beginning, both men gravitated to the English gardening tradition of creating planted "rooms," based on such masterpieces as Sissinghurst and Hidcote Manor, and to the idea of clean lines over which plants can quietly run riot. When they first acquired Hollister House in 1978, they visited Sissinghurst and other English gardens intensively—two or three times a year for several years—and took more than 300 photos so that they could carefully study and plan their garden. "We were especially intrigued by Sissinghurst of the early 1980s," Ron says. "There was a sense of slight decay, with untidy plants and crazy paving—it wasn't so neat." Despite its English inspiration, the garden at Hollister House ends up feeling very American, a result of unexpected plantings and creative responses to the New England climate. "The trick is to have preconceptions," says George, "and fit them into where you are."

As a landscape-architecture student at Cornell in the late 1960s, Ron says he faced "horrifying choices of paving material" and plants "whose most important criterion was whether they could take exhaust." (He quickly switched to fine art, and still paints landscapes, occasionally using the garden room as a studio.) In the past decade American gardening has become more complex, and he and George note the decline of the kidney-shaped bed (a 1950s favorite) with satisfaction.

Both Ron and George offer clues to their distinctive gardening styles. Embedded in Ron's fondness for architectural foundations and due formality is an early memory of following his father, a decorative painter, through the grand houses and grounds of Long Island's Gold Coast before they were opened for the season. Certain ritual acts—the furnishing of gardens every spring with Chinese porcelain, the bedding out, the hinged rose trellises three stories high that were lowered off the wall for painting—still tug at his memory and tickle his imagination. And George's exuberance—he calls Connecticut "the promised land"—comes from a youth spent in the extremes of the Texas climate. "Nothing would grow there. When my first lily bloomed, I rushed everyone outside. The foliage had been scorched black by the sun and there was just one pathetic blossom, in its absolute last gasp." He pauses. "I was ecstatic."

PREVIOUS PAGE: *The garden house opens onto a gravel courtyard, down the slope from the 1760s house.* OPPOSITE: *The garden provides many opportunities for the artist.* ABOVE: *Blue and white bowls, including a large one from Morocco, a yellowware jug, a delft tile, a cast-iron bird house, and assorted lamps, candlesticks, and pots line the shelves of an early American painted cupboard in the garden house.*

TOP RIGHT: *A tree-shaped myrtle topiary augments sketches of urns and flower pots by Ron.* BOTTOM LEFT: *A nineteenth-century blue-and-white Chinese tobacco-leaf garden seat on the bridge offers a tempting spot from which to watch the brook.* BOTTOM RIGHT: *Ron Johnson.*

TOP LEFT: *An* Actinidia kolomikta–*covered doorway in the retaining wall leads to a flat reflecting pool.* TOP RIGHT: *George Schoellkopf.* ABOVE: *The bridge crosses Sprain Brook at a narrow point.* FOLLOWING PAGE: *The garden house is glimpsed at the end of a path planted with hostas, ferns, and* Rosa moyesii, *with an apple tree at left and the formal gray garden at right.*

Country Garden Rooms 45

TOP: *Matching storm lanterns festoon the red bridge, seen here with the main house beyond.* BOTTOM: *A large 'Boule de Neige' rhododendron and a forest of ferns frame the way to the clipped boxwood hedges of the gray garden.*

TOP: *In summer the courtyard garden is dense with colorful plants like* Ornithogalum sandosonii, *agapanthus, and species of mullein.* BOTTOM: *The garden house acts as dining room, resting area, and, as shown here, artist's studio.*

Idyllic Delight

and Detail

When Tommy Simpson and Missy Stevens built their wood-frame house in Washington, Connecticut, ten years ago (with Tommy acting as designer, Missy as general contractor), they carefully incorporated into the plan the august crab apple tree that was already on the site. "The workmen couldn't understand it," laughs Missy. Both artists respect the inherent value of working with what already exists, and they share an ability to make art out of anything they touch. This, coupled with a decidedly offbeat sensibility, has produced a house and gardens filled with quirky details: handmade spokes on the staircase, each turned differently; wooden silhouettes of tiny creatures inserted unexpectedly in the wide floorboards; and a swing carved with the word *Fragonard* hanging from a rafter in the bedroom.

In mid-July the enclosed lower garden (lower only in altitude, Missy points out) is awash in the scent of viburnum. Fuzzy fronds of asparagus wave in the wind. Missy is an active member of the Mad Gardeners, a group of local enthusiasts, and the garden exhibits her wide-ranging interests. Parallel beds filled with mixed plantings of vegetables and flowers run the length of the plot. A small toolshed stands in the middle, with a pergola entwined with clematis, trumpet vine, and honeysuckle at one end of the garden, and a covered seat and eating area at the other. Called "the Italian garden" by Tommy—in homage to the gardening tastes of the Italian families he grew up near as well as out of a "real wish to have a garden in Italy"—this last nook's centerpiece is a blue-stone slab table on a cypress wood base. The covered seat faces the toolshed, the door of

which is decorated with a dozen or so small wooden cow cutouts, and both seat and shed were made from the same weathered barn boards. A green canvas awning can be pulled shut on wires that stretch across the length of the passageway. The gazebo, as Missy and Tommy affectionately call the homely seat, is nestlike, feathered with soft pale cushions that migrated from an old porch swing. By late summer the vines that Missy plants every year have swarmed up the sides and over the top. Protected on one side by paling, on the other by verdant growth, this sheltered spot forms an idyllic garden room.

Both Tommy and Missy are artists with an eye to the unexpected, and both make art that uses (and reuses) fragments of objects meant for other purposes. Missy weaves complexly patterned rugs on a loom—strips of brightly colored corduroy line one wall of her studio—and, her current passion, makes thread paintings, or "miniature embroidered pictures." Tommy paints and sculpts, and also crafts clocks, beds, chairs, and other pieces of furniture out of wood, pierced tin, brushes, and found items. This attitude toward what others might consider junk—broken tools, unraveled baskets, ripped quilts—extends especially to their lower garden. The fence, for example, consists of half-inch-wide saplings that they cut down when they cleared out some woodland on their lot. Scarecrows placed strategically throughout the garden are not just assemblages of objects but personalities, evidence of these artists' knack for breathing life into their creations.

PREVIOUS PAGE: *A herd of wooden cows is tacked up on the door of the toolshed.* OPPOSITE: *A green awning connects the tool house to the gazebo, a covered seat made of the same weathered barn boards.* TOP: *Daisy the cat naps in the birdbath.* BOTTOM: *Missy Stevens and Tommy Simpson.* FOLLOWING PAGE: *The fence surrounding the lower garden consists of saplings that were salvaged from timbered woodland.*

Earthy Comfort

Interior designer Bunny Williams's rooms strike a chord, triggering some memory, or inventing one perhaps, for visitors often respond to places she has decorated with longing and nostalgia. It has something to do with her style, a graceful blend of pale colors and soothing textures enlivened with interesting objects. But it has more to do with the way she makes a room and its parts look as if they have been there forever. This is no less true for her outdoor spaces, whether the design subject is a kitchen garden or a potting shed. "I want to create interior spaces that you want to be in," she says. "It's the same thing for a garden."

Bunny grew up on a farm in Charlottesville, Virginia, among gardeners—her mother was an impassioned flower lover—and though Bunny was more beneficiary than doer ("I don't think you say a ten-year-old child really gardens, do you?"), she always knew that someday she wanted a garden. In fact, this desire prompted her to look for a weekend country house in Connecticut a decade and a half ago. The run-down 1840 Federal-style edifice she found in Falls Village had served as a rooming house. Paint was peeling and plaster flaking off the walls. The house lacked grace and charm; the garden was nonexistent. Over the years Bunny has lovingly resurrected both indoors and out.

Like her wicker-filled screened porch or her salmon-colored front entry, every part of Bunny's garden has a special atmosphere. The mood of the formal beds, framed by gray treillage, is very different from the enclosed vegetable and flower garden, with its arbor of natural locust posts and paths of old brick. Bunny also notes the difference between the act of gardening and the result: *"Gardening*

is what you do, an activity. A *garden* is an intimate space, someplace you want to be."

Bunny converted a room in the old carriage house into the ideal potting shed: moist, grubby, filled with ancient pots and obscure tools, rakes, hoes, bee-skeps, rolls of hemp, watering cans, stakes of all heights and materials. Bunny's professional eye extends, of course, to this aesthetically pleasing and somehow deeply satisfying arrangement of objects, and a stately old American armoire "stores all the things I want out of sight," she laughs. But Bunny's potting shed is not a decorator's folly. It is first and foremost a workspace, where she and her gardener, Debbie Munson, pot up seeds, transplant seedlings, and make notes. It is up to her visitors to indulge in fantasies of hot, indolent summer afternoons spent lounging with a book or daydreaming in the cool, earthy region of Bunny's talent.

PREVIOUS PAGE: *In the kitchen garden, a nineteenth-century Coalbrookdale fern-and-blackberry pattern cast-iron seat holds court underneath the locust pergola.* OPPOSITE: *In the potting shed, Bunny keeps notes on an old school desk beneath a window that overlooks the kitchen garden.* TOP: *The potting shed stores tools, stakes, French cloches, and esoteric gardening paraphernalia such as a section of a wattling fence and a straw bee-skep atop an antique American armoire.* ABOVE RIGHT: *Bunny Williams, photographed at her shop, Treillage.* FOLLOWING PAGE: *The side terrace, with handsome late-1800s French metal garden chairs and a stone table, offers peace and privacy.*

Pastimes and Pleasures

Illustrated Beauty

Jutta Buck is not one to irresponsibly absorb loveliness. As a collector and dealer of botanical prints and drawings in Stamfordville, New York, she craves knowledge as much as beauty, and notes that decorators have misused floral illustrations by making them such an easy decorating choice.

"I have always loved flowers," Jutta says, recollecting the open-air flower markets in the Berlin of her youth. "When I moved to New York in 1965, it was very hard to find fresh, inexpensive flowers. All they had were the icebox variety." Browsing through the boxes of a print shop one day, she discovered a number of floral prints and bought the prettiest to hang on her walls. "At first it was just a way to bring in flowers, but as I studied the subject I became increasingly interested." Virtually every print, whether a hand-colored copper engraving, stipple, mezzotint, or aquatint, comes from an old book that has been cut up, its pages dispersed. And for every printed plate, there exists a piece of original art, usually a watercolor—these became Jutta's specialty. She learned the names of European masters such as Georg Dionys Ehret, Pierre-Joseph Redouté, John Edwards, and Pierre-Antoine Poiteau, artists who all captured the beauty of flowers with an exquisite, formal restraint.

Soon Jutta had covered her walls and crammed her drawers full, too, and the prints themselves were becoming rarer and more expensive. On travels abroad she noticed that prices for botanical prints were much higher in Europe than in the States, and—a familiar story—she began dealing to finance her own collecting. She bought in America and sold in Europe. Then, in the 1980s when

the decorating craze for botanical prints drove the American market up, she sold what she bought in Europe over here.

Jutta's mania for documentation does not stop with her collecting. She has studiously researched the 1780s Stamfordville farmhouse that she and her husband bought in 1982, and in which they've been living full-time since they left Manhattan in 1991. The current living room was attached to the main house in the 1820s and was transformed into a sunroom with the addition in 1915 of an entire wall of "nothing but windows." Today the room overlooks a cottage-style garden planted to provide flowers many months of the year and filled with delphiniums, hollyhocks, and Jutta's favorite old shrub roses. Light streams through the windows, which act as a greenhouse in winter, and sets off the delicious cool blue painted along the wainscot and trim. Simply furnished with an antique desk, chairs, and a soft upholstered couch, the room basks in sun-filled comfort. There are flowers everywhere, painted on porcelain plates and vases, embroidered on an ecclesiastical cape, in engravings, and, of course, in Jutta's collection of botanical paintings, some of which hang on the walls.

Jutta dreams of someday establishing a first-rate collection of botanical paintings for a museum in this country, and laments that so many curators and scholars write off "a vital part of our scientific and cultural history" as merely decorative. In the meantime she sells by appointment, though there are a few cherished pictures she will never part with. Leafing through a Book of Remembrance, a young Victorian woman's album filled with still lifes of shells and pansies, little rhymes and postcards carefully glued in, she smiles and says, "Basically it's a business of love."

PREVIOUS PAGE: *An assortment of botanical illustrations on Jutta's desk includes an eighteenth-century copper engraving by a German artist and a Victorian friendship album.* OPPOSITE: *Flowers in every guise, from potpourri to an embroidered Italian seventeenth-century religious cape, adorn the garden room.* TOP: *A "black" hollyhock from Jutta's garden, one of her favorite flowers, peeks out of a glass vase near an eighteenth-century Dutch watercolor of a tulip.* CENTER: *One of Jutta's prize illustrations is this fine watercolor on vellum of carnations, circa 1840.* RIGHT: *Jutta Buck.*

Collecting Elegance

"I surround myself with plants and flowers," says Barry Ferguson, a noted plantsman and gardener. "They're my medium of expression." Born in New Zealand to "a gardening mama," Barry has designed the aisle decorations and flowers for the Winter Antiques Show at the Seventh Regiment Armory on Park Avenue for twenty-odd years, and he is renowned for his innovative floral arrangements and bouquets. Out in Oyster Bay, New York, Barry inhabits a complex of barn, carriage house, and stable—now a conservatory famed for its exotic specimens. Set in four acres of woodland and once part of the Roosevelt estate, the buildings are all brown and white, and their board-and-batten structure displays "affiliations with the Scandinavian style." The early use of the buildings is hard to guess, however, as the quarters have been redesigned and refined enormously. The hay shaft from the loft, for example, has been turned into a terra-cotta–lined taproom, and the foaling stable acts as Barry's office. Barry himself lives in the carriage house and hands' quarters next to the large stable that once provided shelter for twenty-one horses.

Though Barry always has a supply of green, growing plants and flowers in his rooms, he also surrounds himself with botanical illustrations. He started his collection with "five-shilling specials" purchased in London. Today his bedroom is filled entirely with pictures of auriculas, and the stairwell and upstairs hallways are stacked three and four high with floral watercolors and prints. Though he loves historic renditions, he's especially interested in "the modern eye," and he keeps up a regular stream of commissions from contemporary artists such as

Valentine Lawford, Kevin Nicolay, and Jessica Tcherepnine, often supplying the latter with the plants she is to draw.

Converting a stable or barn into a house poses special problems. For one thing, it's very expensive to heat so much living space. With much double glazing, a new boiler, a new roof, and frequent inspections for termites, however, Barry says, "I'm now in control." He wanted to put down tiles in the carriage house's garden/living room, but because of the underfloor heating, and the distant but real possibility of pipes breaking, he hired decorative painter Fran Dearden to simulate tiles of beige limestone with paint. Dearden went one step further and added a few fallen leaves, pheasant feathers, and other natural artifices such as a bird's nest complete with eggs. Thick wooden shutters, a gift from his friend the late conductor Norman Luboff, seal off the room from winter's cold weather. Two "very brittle" English iron copies of second-century Roman urns house choice plants of the season—"I'm constantly circulating things from the conservatory," he says. Smaller, colorful flowers are arranged in a collection of ancient and modern Chinese ceramic vases on a nineteenth-century French table by the window. Barry's travels throughout the world, and especially in Asia, inform the aesthetic of his garden room. In addition to the vases, there are Chinese kilims on the wall and two elegant Chinese rosewood chairs. "It's very difficult, but I'm trying not to add any more treasures," he says with some regret.

PREVIOUS PAGE: *Barry's complex of buildings nestles in a woodland setting.* OPPOSITE: *The "green room," a utility area, holds Barry's collection of old watering cans.* ABOVE: *Barry Ferguson and his scissors.*

TOP LEFT: *These onions, grown by writer Roald Dahl, were painted by Alastair Gordon.* TOP RIGHT: *A carved wood horse's head denotes the former stable.* BOTTOM LEFT: *The house, decorated with hanging baskets, is surrounded by plants and trees.* BOTTOM RIGHT: *Barry commissioned Kevin Nicolai to paint this watercolor portrait of some favorite auriculas.* OPPOSITE: *Pots of caladiums line the deck.* FOLLOWING PAGE: *The Oriental motif of the garden room incorporates kilims on the wall, lacquer vases filled with roses on the table, and two rosewood chairs. The floor has been hand-painted to resemble tiles.*

Eccentric Retreat

Robert Jackson's trompe l'oeil paintings are miraculous, tricking the eye, as of course they should, and lulling the unsuspecting into vistas of grandeur. One of the most talented decorative painters at work today, Robert has painted walls inspired by a Russian palace for Bunny Williams's design for the Kips Bay Decorator Show House, as well as a garden landscape for the garden room of Blair House, the four-story mansion across from the White House used to house foreign dignitaries, where he also created sitting and dining room panoramas of views of Washington. Throughout Strawberry Hill, Horace Walpole's house near London, Robert re-created the Gothic Revival style, one of his particular favorites. When he's not working on a commission, he paints botanical watercolors for pleasure.

During the ten years Robert lived in London as an expatriate Canadian, he became enamored of gardening, and when he moved to the United States, he settled in a rambling 1890 farmhouse where he could put down roots. Situated neatly on the edge of a hill near Germantown, New York, the house commands a view of the Catskill Mountains but has enough level ground for a substantial perennial garden. First Robert built a barn, an elegant gray-blue clapboard building with arched windows, and then in 1980 he added on a studio to the main house, giving him space and the proper light to work. The studio has a northern exposure, always desirable to artists because the light provides few shadows and is the least variable. Presided over by a "too efficient" Norwegian stove, the room is an odd mixture—part early-nineteenth-century artist's atelier, part naturalist's

den. There's something wonderfully eccentric in its furnishings: an English Regency library chair with caned armrests; a French wrought-iron café table; a majestic celadon-green screen. A wide, white bookcase that Robert fashioned using a pair of 1800s columns holds his library, books relating to the arts, gardening, and natural history that he consults regularly for research and inspiration. The floor, a pickled checkerboard of pale blue and cream, is quite American, whereas an unexpected park bench against one wall feels distinctly Edwardian. A potted fig gets moved in and out depending on the weather.

If the wall holding the library is intimate and old-fashioned, its facing wall is dramatic, offering a view of the garden stretching away into purple mountains. A third wall displays a set of framed Jackson watercolors, while the final wall, streaked with the ghosts of former murals, forms an abstract art work of its own. (Robert paints on easels and on canvases attached directly to the wall.) Taken altogether, the components of this studio/garden room are enigmatic, proplike, and as artfully arranged as one of the artist's works. But in addition to the leafy plants that he is so fond of painting, Robert keeps his tools, pots, and clippers near the door so that he can go straight into the garden for a bit of tending. The light and proximity to the borders make the room ideal for horticultural tasks, which in turn engender further creative visions, an arrangement that is both pleasant and practical.

PREVIOUS PAGE: *The studio wall retains the remnants of finished paintings.* *Redouté's* Oaks of America *and André Michaux's* North America Sylva, OPPOSITE AND BOTTOM RIGHT, *are some of the natural history books, here festooned with acorns, that inspire Robert's botanical paintings.* TOP RIGHT: *A park bench beside a fig tree brings an air of the outdoors in.*

Pastimes and Pleasures 79

80 The Garden Room

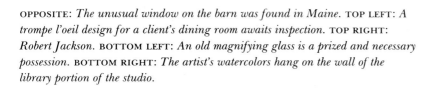

OPPOSITE: *The unusual window on the barn was found in Maine.* TOP LEFT: *A trompe l'oeil design for a client's dining room awaits inspection.* TOP RIGHT: *Robert Jackson.* BOTTOM LEFT: *An old magnifying glass is a prized and necessary possession.* BOTTOM RIGHT: *The artist's watercolors hang on the wall of the library portion of the studio.*

Pastimes and Pleasures 81

Moyesii

Cydonia Mauleii

LE JARDINIER

20 des Plantes qu'il a semées sur couches,
Cloches en avançant aussi beaucoup
végétation : elles sont faites à l'imita
d'une Cloche de fonte ; elles ont envi
un pied & demi de largeur par le ba
leur ouverture, & autant de haute
avec un gros bouton aussi de verre p
les prendre & les placer commodeme
il s'en fait quelquefois de plus gran
On fait aussi des Cloches de Paille ; e
sont propres pour couvrir les Plantes no
veillement transplantées, afin de les ga
rantir des ardeurs du soleil qui les déc
roit.

d'une Fourche de fer p
oder les fumiers do
ches : un Jardin
cet outil lui e
composé d'un
chons ou bra
arbées en d
environ un pied
l'emmanche d'un bâton long, de trois
quatre pieds.

Un Jardinier Fleuriste ne doit point
non plus manquer de Truelle ; c'est à l'a
de de cet outil qu'il leve en motte heu
reusement ses Plantes, La Truelle est con
posée d'un manche de bois, d'un colle
& d'une feuille de bois ou de fer chai
& large.

Corniola
nautica.

Literary Presence

"I always knew I wanted to live in Maine," says Pamela Logan, who bought her house near Ogunquit the day after she saw it advertised in *Down East Magazine*. "I hadn't even seen the inside, but I could feel it was right." The house, part of which is an old tavern, had had only one owner, a woman whose story of heartbreak and fortitude might have appeared in Sarah Orne Jewett's *Country of the Pointed Firs* or one of the other Maine classics Pamela adores. "She was a North Carolina woman on vacation who fell in love with a local. They planned to marry and she began building the house in 1932 as a sort of love nest perched on the coast." (A carving on the kitchen door has their initials in a heart.) "But just as the house was being completed, the love affair ended tragically." Pamela sighs. "The woman lived here alone until she was ninety-three." Enclosed in a private green space with an old millstone, a wellstone, and granite slabs giving definition to the well-tended lawn, the clapboard house hardly seems the site of tragedy. In fact, it emanates happy domesticity. But a narrow, twisting path framed by vigorous rugosa roses opens onto a cove formed by two jutting extensions of rocks and a sudden expanse of sky and sea, and in the romantic wildness of Rose Cove you sense the rugged, poignant beauty that shapes so many of Maine's inhabitants.

The sense of an extraordinary presence still pervades the house, though now it's Pamela's. The low-ceilinged rooms are painted in warm, murky colors—raspberry puree, bluestone gray—and furnished with comfortable armchairs and sofas, upholstered in faded chintzes and English-country-house-style patterns,

creating a lovely counterpoint to the cool, misty Maine air and astonishing white light that intensifies reds and yellows.

Pamela's garden room is a screened-in porch with a brick floor, part of the original house, where she has afternoon tea. Wicker furniture, with cushions colored to match old brick and weathered wood, makes the room a good place for lounging on summer afternoons. Though you can't actually see the water from the room, which looks out onto the fenced-in garden designed by Pamela's friend Nancy McCabe, the sense of the sea pervades the setting, in the moist air and changing sky, and in the overall aesthetic. Adjacent is a mudroom crammed with sou'westers, rubber boots, fishing tackle, rods, baskets, and wide-brimmed straw hats. Seashells lie scattered on tables and in boxes in all the rooms.

Pamela came to gardening through books, which she cherishes perhaps more than anything else she collects. (Her favorite book as a child was *No School Today,* a story about being out in the yard.) With the help of gardener Tony Elliott, Pamela has a beautiful, abundant garden, but her most rewarding acts of gardening take place in her mind, when she reads about hedges or beekeeping or tools. "Books are marvelous," she says, "because they lead you down any path." *The Treasury of Flowers* by Alice M. Coats introduced her to the world of tiny, jewellike botanical illustrations, now an area of passionate interest. Pamela turned a small room, a passageway almost, into a library and filled it with precious first editions and rare botanical tomes, including an 1821 *Histoire des Tulipes* by Charles Malo, with

engravings by Pancrace Bessa painted in color, and Charlotte de Latour's 1833 hand-colored *Le Langage des Fleurs* and *Queen of Flowers,* or *Memoirs of the Rose,* the latter with hand-colored plates by James Andrews. Other favorites are a complete set of Vita Sackville-West's collected articles, and, "for pure pleasure," the works of Beverley Nichols, the British writer whose description of his own garden room appears in *A Thatched Roof.* "In the long winters here," Pamela explains, "if you can't read, you're done for."

PREVIOUS PAGE: *Exquisite hand-colored volumes such as a 1754* Le Jardinièr *and an 1839* The Floral Calendar *are some of Pamela's favorite books.* OPPOSITE: *Assorted hats, fishing baskets and gear, Wellingtons, and sou'westers gather in the mud room.* TOP: *Yum Yum, the pug, naps near an 1852 copy of* The Queen of Flowers. RIGHT: *An illustration of auriculas in an 1822 copy of* On the Culture of Flowers *complements some of the originals.*

TOP LEFT: *Tucked in the garden are glass cloches and bronze animals; an energetic frog leaps atop the fence post at left.* TOP RIGHT: *A collection of greenhouses includes one fashioned in lead.* BOTTOM LEFT: *Tea in the garden room is enhanced by an early-1800s Wedgwood tea service depicting insects, moths, and flowers.* BOTTOM RIGHT: *Pamela converted a passageway into a small library packed with enticing literary and gardening finds.*

TOP: *Nancy McCabe designed the outdoor furniture for Pamela's garden.*
BOTTOM LEFT: *Pamela Logan and her pugs, Yoda and Yum Yum, relax in the garden.* BOTTOM RIGHT: *The wavy edges of a Parrot tulip in a crocus pot echo the shapes of shells from the beach. The Prussian-school painting of fruit and insects dates from 1690.* FOLLOWING PAGES: *Pamela and her pugs sit in splendor amid tulips; the garden is a summer delight.*

Black tulips for the bride

Pamela Ogunquit

2⅞"Ⅰ maine

Scrapbook

Aesthetic

"Everyone thought I was out of my mind to buy this house," garden designer Nancy McCabe says of her squat 1790 stucco house in Falls Village, Connecticut, probably once owned by somebody who ran the canal across the road. "It was definitely on the wrong side of the tracks. But I just adored it." The trim gray house with green shutters evokes some country vicar's parsonage, with a kitchen garden surrounded by espaliered fruit trees by the back door and roosters roaming the front terrace. Nancy's greenhouse juts off the kitchen; there's a tree house tucked up on the hillside; and the sunken terrace garden she devised is in the spirit of an Annapolis mansion she admired as a girl.

Nancy grew up under the thumb of her father, a fanatic azalea and camellia man, and made her first garden—devoted to violets—when she was ten or twelve. During the years she was trying to be a painter, she found it more rewarding to garden, and she gradually began to spend her time planting and designing. "I never intended to design gardens professionally," Nancy says, but when decorator John Saladino saw the window boxes she had made for her husband's bookstore, the Lion's Head in nearby Salisbury, he hired her to plan his own garden and spread the word to friends. She's since created gardens for Kevin Bacon, William Paley, and Mrs. John D. Rockefeller IV.

Nancy studied art and art history in college, and this background has proved invaluable for her horticultural designs—"I've seen the gardens of the Medici, as painted by Utens"—but her two real loves are gardening and collecting. Nancy's particular talent lies in her ability to add an unexpected dimension to all her

PREVIOUS PAGE: *Muted colors and soft fabrics radiate warmth and comfort in the garden room.* TOP RIGHT: *A rare early-nineteenth-century Wedgwood soup bowl is shown with a tiny ivory-handled spade.* BOTTOM LEFT: *Nancy writes often in her gardening notebook.* BOTTOM RIGHT: *A pearlware cup and saucer date from the early 1800s.*

creations, whether in a garden or an interior, bringing beauty to the most mundane situations. She talks of keeping bees, for instance, yet the hive she has in mind is no ordinary wooden box but a white and gold apiary in the manner of those crafted for royal Parisian bees. And in a corner of her kitchen, a west highland white terrier snoozes on a kingly dog bed invented by Nancy, its chin settled on a tuft of the toile cushion, its hind feet wedged against the elaborate frame of the pagoda-esque backdrop.

In the garden room, whose door opens wide on the green lawn, Nancy points to the curtains that she made from a beloved childhood dress sewn for her by her mother. The valances consist of four pieces of early needlework, each decorated with old roses and a small square house, that she and her husband found when they decided to buy the house, as well as a strip of ancient French ribbon bought in New York. After they had hung the curtains on Victorian brass rods, they found a matching finial up in the attic, yet another sign, says Nancy, that they were meant to live there. The palette she favors is pale and dusty, drawn from floral prints and old faded fabrics. "I'm attracted toward earth colors," she admits. "I like the color of mud."

The garden room has a kind of scrapbook aesthetic, especially since each item is awash in associations: on the couch rests a needlepoint pillow made by her grandmother; aquatints from Robert Thornton's *The Temple of Flora* and other seventeenth- and eighteenth-century prints and botanical illustrations hang on the walls; a sunflower clock ticks across the room. The bookshelves are lined with rows of the garden books and pottery she has collected since she was twenty-four. She tends to "gravitate to the warmth of early soft paste pottery," although she has also collected later patterns relating to flowers and the garden. Nancy's interests are eclectic, but what unites these objects, whether watering cans, hose heads, prints, dishes, or a marvelous needlepoint rug, is her criterion for collecting: "the way it touches the heart."

TOP: *Playing cards cover the face of a nineteenth-century French clock.* RIGHT: *Nancy McCabe.* FOLLOWING PAGES: *Nancy's collection includes a cherished old book and a pearlware jug illustrated with farming implements.*

Botanical Study

As a child Jessica Tcherepnine painted flowers in her parents' garden, near Gravetye Manor, William Robinson's house and famous garden in Sussex, England. Today she is one of a small group of internationally respected botanical illustrators. Apart from three very significant months as a twenty-year-old at the studio of one Signora Simi in Florence, the recent winner of two Royal Horticultural Society gold medals for a series of watercolors has had no formal artistic or botanical training. "You just keep on looking until you get it right," she explains. Although botanical illustration differs from flower painting in that its aim is accurate representation of the plant, it is no less of an art, and Jessica collects the watercolors of her contemporaries, all of whom have an individual style within the genre. Jessica's own paintings are delicately shaded, precise renderings of irises, anemones, daylilies, and so forth. Because each watercolor can take several weeks to create, she looks carefully in her own and her friends' gardens before deciding on an example of a plant in bud and bloom, seeking one that won't die or fade too quickly—accurate representation of leaf and blossom color is essential. The winter months are naturally more fallow, although horticultural friends with greenhouses, such as "superflorist" Barry Ferguson, offer her tempting specimens.

In 1983, Jessica decided to leave the New York auction house Christie's, where she had worked in the Oriental department, in order to paint full-time. Since then she has spent each summer at the Victorian house she and her husband own in Millbrook, New York. Planted in the 1930s with an array of fruit

trees—including apples, cherries, quinces, and others—the grounds are a shower of blossoms, and provide much material for the studio every spring.

Though Jessica is embarking on a series of peach, plum, and apple paintings, many picked from her own garden, she is also intrigued by more exotic forms, such as tropical fruits from the West Indies. She makes annual trips to Nives to paint akee and the like. "I'm beginning to think really pretty flowers can be overdone," she says. "Unusual and grotesque shapes are often more interesting." As examples she cites the dead flowers, especially sunflowers, and cracked seed pods she paints in the winter. "I love doing dead flowers. Often they make a stronger image."

Several years ago Jessica and her husband added on a room to the north end of the house, painstakingly designed to be in keeping with the rest of the gabled, white clapboard building. Used in summer as their living room, the space is simply one in which to enjoy the garden. "It's a very English idea," she says. "I suppose it looks less like a traditional garden room than it might because we wanted to fit it in with the house." Her own parents had had an informal "sun" room where the family ate dinner from time to time. "It was very utilitarian," says Jessica, "with a big oak table and trugs, tools, and muddy boots lying about." The Tcherepnine garden room is far neater, with a polished floor, clean French doors painted white on the inside and green on the outside, and pretty upholstered furniture. On overcast days she paints in the garden room, which functions as an intermediate area between the outdoors and the rest of the house.

On the coldest days of winter, the family retreats to the stone hearth of the main living room. But during the remainder of the year the bright, window-filled room allows Jessica to enjoy her plants, relieved of the intense concentration her art demands.

PREVIOUS PAGE: *The garden room is set up as a studio with the necessary equipment for botanical painting. Three studies painted by Jessica include,* OPPOSITE, *the skunk cabbage of North America;* TOP, *akee of the West Indies; and* BOTTOM, Angelica gigas. CENTER, *Jessica Tcherepnine carefully examines the characteristics of the common milkweed before beginning to paint.*

Garden Room Fantasies

Meditations

in Green

"I'm not a gardener in the traditional sense," fashion designer Bill Blass explains. "I like to decorate my gardens with things I would use in rooms." His lovely weekend house in New Preston, Connecticut, is uncluttered, comfortable, and appointed with a few items of historical interest, such as a set of maps of the continents originally drawn for Louis XVI and a group of medallions of Roman emperors. Bill has applied the same principles outdoors to create a series of rooms—or, more properly, settings, since these spaces have neither walls nor ceilings—that are conducive to meditation and reflection. Though open and verdant, these spaces are similar in spirit and mood to his interiors. In an allée of trees redolent of pine, for example, six unidentified but distinguished ancient thinkers perch on stone pedestals. Despite its distinctly sylvan setting, this allée has the dignity of a well-furnished gallery, and its proportions are such that a stroll feels comfortably domestic.

When Bill bought the house, an old tavern used as a Revolutionary meeting place after 1776, he loved the twenty-two acres of wooded landscape behind it and made an effort to create a park "that looks as if it happened naturally," he says. "It was a matter of editing the mass of trees rather than replanting." Although there is a totally separate cutting garden filled with bright flowers for the house, Bill says, "I wanted there to be stretches with no color visible other than green." And most of the garden achieves a simplicity of form and color—grass and trees—the better to highlight his eclectic assortment of old terra-cotta and marble sculptures.

In a nook in the woods, a mossy, weatherworn group of limbless terra-cotta gentlemen and one headless lady soundlessly serenades. The quartet, made as part of a frieze for John Nash's opera house in Haymarket, represents the "Origin and Progress of Music" and had lived at the Tate and Castle Howard before Bill brought them over from England. Also buried in the woods for wandering guests to happen upon is a very rare set of early-nineteenth-century rustic garden furniture, a table and chairs that look as if they had been hewn from the surrounding trees. (The pieces are actually made of reconstituted stone.) Other treasures include a nineteenth-century copy of Bertel Thorvaldsen's statue *Lion of Lucerne,* set into a drywall fence; a heavy lead cistern imprinted with the bust of George III; and a thatched gazebo built by carpenter Jeffrey Cayle and placed on a stone outcropping.

A glimpse of white modernity beckons at the end of one of the long grassy walks. A massive bench, done in the manner of Chippendale, sits solidly before some bushes. To its right is a marble medallion crafted by Yugoslav sculptor Igor Mitoraj that plays with references to the Italian Renaissance. Here is the place to sit and ponder the source of Bill's inspiration for his down-to-earth couture. Like heaven on earth, Bill's garden room is not so much a place as a state of mind.

PREVIOUS PAGE: *A classical wooden sculpture looks down the long vista to a white Chippendale-style bench.* OPPOSITE: *The surviving remnant of a frieze depicts the "Origin and Progress of Music."* TOP: *Bill Blass.* CENTER: *A feathered visitor perches on the wall.* BOTTOM: *A piece by Igor Mitoraj emerges from the foliage.* FOLLOWING PAGE: *An ancient thinker stands in the philosopher's walk.*

Temple Folly

Artist and garden designer Hitch Lyman has always been moved by notions of antiquity, making pilgrimages to Athens and elsewhere to paint classical ruins. "I used to make lists of the things I like to paint—bridges, ruins, out-of-season tavernas, olive trees, and so forth," he says. "Then I realized my theme was places where you know you would be happy." One such place is the 1840 Greek Revival house he inhabits in Trumansburg, New York, a rural area that he describes as "rich just before the Civil War, poor ever since, and littered with temples." Hitch's evocative watercolors have a gallant air, at once precise and nostalgic. He approaches his own landscape with the same panache, creating spots and vistas suggestive of other things, places both familiar and strange.

After buying the house three years ago, Hitch thought he might enjoy having a classical folly in the garden and put out word that he was looking for columns. Two weeks later someone offered him four from a porch that was being torn down. He bought them for twenty-five dollars, drew up plans, and hired two carpenters to produce the temple. The bottom four inches of each wood column had rotted, so his team simply cut down the pedestals; the result is columns that are much heavier than those on the main house, and more in keeping with archaic Greek Doric examples, which don't have bases. The temple is divided in two, with the back section serving as a potting shed that opens onto the garden; the front room is meant for dining, though so far Hitch has used it more for musing than for eating. He painted the walls with an unfinished mural of a nineteenth-century view of the European landscape—a "pre-impressionist pastiche" in the manner

of Poussin or Corot of "a landscape I'd like to live in." The reference sounds quite cultured until he confesses that it's really just to amuse visitors: his true inspiration was Rex Whistler, the mannered English artist who illustrated garden writer Beverley Nichols's books. Inside, the temple is empty but for the stove and gravel floor. Hitch tends to "sit on the porch and stare at the pond." At night in the rain, the house lights reflected on the pond remind him of Venice.

When he bought the house, it was set down in the middle of a field, much as it might have been when it was first built. He has steadily been landscaping, discreetly planting oaks and beeches ("I wish they would grow," he moans), yews, boxwood, magnolias, and white redbud so that the trees won't disturb the impression of a wild meadow. A terrace off the house intersperses fieldstones among the flowers. Here, the poppy bed, started by scattering a bag of seeds in gravel, is bordered with linden trees and interplanted with old roses, hyacinths, and sweet violets in spring and evening-scented stock later in the summer.

In Hitch's lexicon, favorite plants are "weeds" (sometimes "edible weeds"), and rocks "bear scars"—the slabs paving his terrace, for instance, are field-scavenged and marked by "men working on earth with iron." His comments disguise an attitude that is almost Romantic in nature, a yearning for places and experiences that are grander, more profound and fulfilling than the quotidian, and this desire, in turn, produces an ability to perceive his surroundings more acutely. Keenly aware that "ours is a very gray landscape," Hitch pur-

chased a pound of the yellow ocher used to paint local buildings the last time he was in Greece. When it came time to paint the temple, he mixed a little of the pigment into the white he had chosen, and now "it always looks like it's sunny over there."

PREVIOUS PAGE: *Inside, the garden temple has a gravel-covered floor, wood-burning stove, and "half-finished mural" on the wall. The template for the balcony balustrades is on the floor.* OPPOSITE: *A solitary chair on the temple's portico provides a view to the main house.* TOP: *Classical ruins are one of Hitch's favorite watercolor subjects.* BOTTOM: *An antique wooden Chinese bowl, a souvenir from Hitch's travels, is shown with the garden house in the distance.*

TOP LEFT AND RIGHT: *Hitch Lyman at home and as traveler.* BOTTOM LEFT:
The artist's hat, pen, and ink are spread before his design of the temple. BOTTOM
RIGHT: *Dinner—a bowl of shrimp—awaits cooking in the garden.* OPPOSITE:
Ivan's watercolor of the temple catches the poppies in bloom. FOLLOWING PAGES:
The temple rises above a field of poppies; a motto graces the garden house door.

Hitch

Ithaca, New York state –

Le temple est blanc.
où amarrées au champ
des coquelicots habitent
des mélancolies athéniennes
17ᵗʰ JUNE

A World

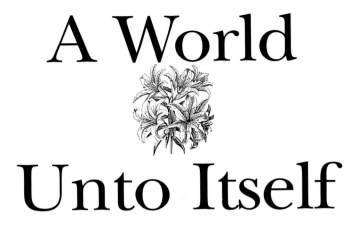

Unto Itself

"If you think about it," says Phyllis Meshover, a psychoanalyst, "gardening is a very basic impulse. It's what man has always done: to take something wild and civilize it." Since 1985, she and her husband, artist Michael Steiner, have cultivated a neglected wreck into a plush, tended sanctuary that is both visually stimulating and spiritually satisfying. Once the estate of a gentleman farmer, the Steiner compound in Roxbury, Connecticut, comprises nine buildings, including the main house, several studio-barns for Michael's work, a greenhouse, and a small cottage, now Phyllis's reading and garden room. "We saw a lot of beautiful places, but this felt like a whole little world unto itself," says Phyllis, recalling the decision to purchase the property. "In fact, it was the special feeling—an illusion, of course—of being in our own universe that convinced us."

"I'm more an eye," says Michael, reflecting on the teamwork that has shaped this remarkably solid illusion. "I comment on form and color. Phyllis is a peasant. She likes to dig." Not surprising, given Phyllis's profession. Freud called psychoanalysis the "archaeology of the mind." But psychoanalysis is not only the business of excavating and unraveling—it's also an act of creation, of linking and encouraging connections. In other words, it's akin to gardening, if this is not too fanciful a comparison. What, then, would one expect the garden of an analyst to be? Not overly tidy, certainly, and marked by a certain passivity—a wait-and-see attitude —but ultimately governed by a hand that knows what to cultivate, when to control, and when to nip something in the bud. Phyllis's garden, at any rate, is easygoing and abundant, filled with loose-limbed plants and determined wisteria. "I

don't actually think about my garden," she confesses. "I use it as a refuge from the cerebral aspects of life." At most, she characterizes it as something "delicate and free."

A few paving stones interspersed among malva, coreopsis, and daylilies lead the way to her garden room. Originally built as a children's playhouse by the gentleman farmer, it is a miniature version of the main house, fashioned with the same white clapboard, neat black shutters, and functioning brick chimney. The inside is not as precious as its exterior might suggest. For one thing, the deeply stained, rough window frames suggest brutish rusticity rather than pastoral charm. And the original wallpaper—now-faded scenes of energetic white-trousered and red-jacketed men running after balls with sticks—is more bewildering than quaint, slightly somber for all its cheerfulness. Yet something about the mixture of playfulness and seriousness in this little library transported to an elf's cottage perfectly captures Phyllis. The room is decisively furnished, like a well-organized mind comfortable with itself: a sturdy leather chair, a wooden table, the necessary volumes (Freud, Eleanor Roosevelt), and a few random objects ready to spark the imagination.

For Phyllis, gardening is "an extremely personal experience"; for Michael, though he is, in Phyllis's words, a "good tender," it is more abstract. His work demands uncluttered environments. The strong steel lines of his sculptures look best placed on wooden boards set into the lawn—just that, green grass, blue sky, and metal—or posed, somewhat enigmatically, within the glass and steel confines of the greenhouse. Michael's and Phyllis's different interests complement each other so well that the gardens and buildings flow successfully into one another, with the result being a paradisiacal world "created very much for us."

PREVIOUS PAGE: *Michael Steiner's metal sculptures punctuate the compound.*
OPPOSITE: *The garden house is mainly a reading room, with a French Art Deco leather chair and original 1930s wallpaper.* ABOVE: *The restored 1930s Lord and Burnham greenhouse retains its traditional pulley system.*

les sculptures en bronze
disposées dans le jardin
brillent sous la pluie.
il y avait aussi
Maillol, Rodin & Barye.

chez Michael Sculptor
Roxbury
Connecticut

OPPOSITE AND TOP: *Inside the glass and steel confines of the greenhouse, one of Michael's sculptures is poised like an edgy animal.* LEFT: *Michael Steiner and Phyllis Meshover.* ABOVE: *A garden of malva, daylilies, irises, foxgloves, bleeding heart, and lady's mantle visually connects the garden house with the greenhouse.*

Garden Room Fantasies 123

Enchanted Barn

Michael Trapp deals in architectural fragments, but his true calling could be set design, for he brings to all his rooms, and even, for that matter, to the simplest table arrangements, a dramatic exuberance, a sense of inventing space and redefining decor. Partly this is due to his materials—cornices, stumps of marble, pilasters, with their connotations of romantic ruins—but mainly it is due to his vision, a combination of the grand gesture and fearlessness, and an ability to find beauty in the unexpected. His colors, luminous blues and grays, suggest dilapidated frescoes and ancient water-streaked walls in forgotten manor houses. The ambiance he creates has at once the theatricality of center stage and the hesitant anticipation of the wings.

Michael grew up in Ohio, the son of gardening parents whose behavior, he hints, bordered on the obsessive. His mother was secretary of the international ivy society, while his German father believed in "a place for everything and everything in its place, with no room for confusion, especially in the lawn." In fact, Michael swears that his father's "reason for having children was lawn maintenance" and recounts weekends spent dethatching and weeding in pursuit of the perfect green turf. His own, emphatically lawnless garden is both structured and riotous, dotted with columns, capitals, and a mossy Victorian fountain. After studying architecture and landscape design, Michael moved east, eventually settling in Connecticut's West Cornwall several years ago. Here he converted a meandering Greek Revival house into a shop, selling pilasters, friezes, urns, cornices, and other architectural fragments, with exotically decorated living quarters

above. The porcelain bathtub, for instance, which lies beneath draped sheets of fabric and is surrounded by nineteenth-century statuary and plants, could stage its own passion play.

Using the same resourcefulness, Michael transformed a small barn at the end of the garden into an enchanted, airy garden house. The original structure, post and beam, is eighteenth century in style, though the building is actually early nineteenth century. "They were just a little provincial here," he explains. Michael replaced the existing windows with large arched windows from the former Rhode Island statehouse and small arches originally belonging to an eighteenth-century meetinghouse. (Most of Michael's finds come over the telephone—"people call me because I've been handling things no one else wanted for so many years.") The windows not only provide a wonderful view of the swirling river below, but also turn the space into a lush "winter hangout" for his potted plants. "It's more effective than a greenhouse," says Michael, "because it maintains an even temperature and is always cool and moist."

Inside, the unevenly tinted walls are a backdrop for Michael's collection of idiosyncratic furniture. The roughness of the interior belies a certain number of amenities, such as heat, electricity, running water, and even a small kitchen and bathroom, hidden behind a "James Bond–type panel." Though these conveniences enable Michael to serve dinner to a dozen friends, the barn retains an abandoned quality that makes dinner by candlelight a small adventure. "It's exciting to leave your house for dinner," says Michael, "even if it's a close commute."

PREVIOUS PAGE: *The 1810 Roman neoclassical fountain in the garden glistens in the sunlight.* OPPOSITE: *An Italian mid-nineteenth-century headless plaster statue and a collection of apples lend ambience.* TOP: *The barn is seen from the main house, with a reflecting pool in the foreground.* BOTTOM: *The barn's walls were painted to resemble worn, weathered boards.*

Garden Room Fantasies 127

TOP LEFT: *Michael Trapp.* TOP RIGHT: *Steps and columns lead down to the river.* BOTTOM LEFT: *A large classical capital, one of several, is the site for potted plants.* BOTTOM RIGHT: *The garden house windows came from the Rhode Island statehouse.* OPPOSITE: *Still lifes, against a background of apple-green walls, accentuate every corner.* FOLLOWING PAGE: *Louis-Philippe chairs, silk shawls, and an 1850s French chandelier create a mood of exotic opulence.*

Forgotten Places

Looking out at his seven perfectly weeded, perfectly edged large flower beds, Peter Wooster can verge on the crotchety. "People who say they like the blowsy look in gardens," he pronounces, "are just lazy." As an interior designer, he's particular; as a gardener, he's a self-proclaimed maintenance fanatic. Peter began his fenced-in garden in Roxbury, Connecticut, in 1986 by marking plots on the grass with string, stakes, and a ruler. He determined early on that "there are too many people who hate too many plants" and decided he would grow as many different plants as he could, in the most challenging color and shape combinations he could think of: marigolds and cockscomb, for example. His plant list contains anything "big-scale, large-leaved, gaudy, and vaguely Victorian": cannas, daturas, amaranths, castor beans, thistles, and heracleum. "Ugly plants thrill me," he says. In high summer Peter's garden becomes a room unto itself, with tall-growing grasses, four corners of eight-foot-high chamaecyparis (an idea stolen from Sissinghurst), and poles covered with morning glory, honeysuckle, and clematis surrounding a shingled umbrella.

Under the shade of an oak, directly across the lawn from the compact main house, sits the Thunder House, a squat one-room structure where Peter sometimes sleeps in the summer. The building, painted barn red, had been a toolshed so filled with "garbage" that it took two years to empty. Peter added a few small-paned square windows and a new door; he also screened off one end and half of both sides for better airflow. The shed's old doors remain permanently closed, fastened with a rusted candelabrum. The furnishings are simple: a flea-market

bed painted green and a chair for midnight musings. A book by the bedside provides a summer's worth of leisurely reading by candlelight. The little house feels like a place in which to fall asleep listening to the crickets or watching the flickering sky beset by summer storms, and then awakening to sunrises over green fields stretching into woods.

The barn is an altogether different matter. Sited deep in the woods and looking as if it had grown there, or at the very least fallen out of the sky (the trees are only six inches away), the barn was built in 1988. The outside consists of weathered boards and old doors, as if it had been around for decades. The inside looks even older, with an ancient daybed, a creaky iron woodstove, a lumpy loft bed, and a few desolate chairs. If the Thunder House is solitary romance, the barn, like some eighteenth-century English eccentric's vision of a picturesque hermit's cave, is bleak exoticism. "One doesn't sleep there alone," says Peter. There is something magical here, a sense of being forgotten, of time passing. Peacefulness pervades this strange place.

For someone so finicky, as prickly at times as the Scotch thistle that grows in his garden, Peter manages to create the most soothing environments. Not only does he reduce a room to its essentials—a bed, a chair— but he imbues it with an extraordinary ambiance, blending whimsy with something more powerful, the recognition of rightness. Peter's garden rooms are deeply satisfying because they are fantasies tinged with wistfulness. For who doesn't yearn to wake up as young and fresh as the new day, to be transported back to a more innocent time?

PREVIOUS PAGE: *The Thunder House was transformed from a shed into a summer sleeping room.* OPPOSITE: *A weathered door opens into the barn's sun-dappled interior.* TOP: *The barn's furniture consists of Appalachian tables, Adirondack chairs, an "extremely short" eighteenth-century bed that has been turned into a daybed, and a range of rustic stools.* BOTTOM: *Stairs lead to an open loft.*

TOP LEFT: *Peter Wooster and Betty the cat.* TOP RIGHT: *The dominant piece of furniture in the Thunder House is a flea market bed.* BOTTOM LEFT AND RIGHT: *Details in the Thunder House are evocative.* OPPOSITE: *A watercolor impression shows the exterior of the Thunder House.* FOLLOWING PAGES: *A collection of American birds' eggs and an eighteenth-century statue of St. Sebastian are some of Peter's finds.*

THE THUNDER HOUSE

Time and Privacy

Terrace in

Summertime

One of the legendary fashion and portrait photographers of the twentieth century, Horst P. Horst is renowned for his stylish, principally black-and-white images that capture, and sometimes create, a glittering world of drama and extravagant gesture. Though born in Germany, Horst lived in Paris for many years, first working at the studio of Le Corbusier, and then at *Vogue* as a photographer. A series of portraits in the 1930s of the luminaries of the day—from Coco Chanel to Gertrude Stein—is probably his most famous work, and his name will forever suggest the glamour of that alluring era.

Horst's more private passion is nature, in all its forms, which he has photographed spectacularly. In 1946 he published *Patterns From Nature,* a collection of closely seen plants, the camera illuminating the textures of bark, petal, leaf, and fiber. In the 1950s he began experimenting with color photography, arranging lush floral still lifes set off by an unexpected object or two. These luscious images verge on the lurid, as full of intensity and emotion as his earlier works were of mystery and intrigue.

Horst's unimposing house in Oyster Bay, New York, mixes his two worlds —the glitter of celebrities and the serenity of nature. Bought after World War II (Horst moved to the United States for good in 1935), the large property had been part of the park surrounding the estate of jeweler Louis Comfort Tiffany, who inhabited a "Turkish palazzo." The landscape still retains a parklike feel, with five allées originating from a clipped evergreen center and two streams joining into a pond with a waterfall. A magnificent pair of copper beeches was given to Horst

by his friend Countess Mona von Bismarck. The house, a small, white, wooden bungalow Horst based on a Tunisian design, is set down as a detail amid the greenery. "With the passage of time," Horst's longtime friend Valentine Lawford wrote in 1966, "his house has assumed the elegance and distinction of an eighteenth-century hunting lodge." Here he created some of his earliest fashion shoots for American *Vogue*, posing models in bathing suits on raffia mats. One of the main attractions, however, is the pergola-covered terrace where he photographed many of his friends: there are snapshots of Edith and Osbert Sitwell, and the back and side of Greta Garbo, who came to lunch that day and refused to have her face photographed; poses of Katharine Hepburn and Jane Fonda lounging in wicker chairs several decades apart; and, more recently, British artists Gilbert & George. Coco Chanel, Truman Capote, Christopher Isherwood, Erich Maria Remarque, Christian Dior, and Billy Baldwin all visited.

The terrace itself is vaguely Mediterranean in feel, fitted with white sailcloth curtains and batik print cloths. A long, low plaster window seat and some smaller benches are permanent pieces of furniture and complement the rattan chairs. Horst uses the terrace as a living room all summer long, setting out carpets on the flagstones and cushions in strategic resting spots. No matter the season, there are always plants, and in summer, climbing roses, morning glories, and other flowering vines drape themselves up the columns and over the pergola. But for all its North African air, there's a freshness and lack of theatricality to the porch, indicative of the peaceful spirit that

reigns there. Horst has been as active as ever of late, with shows in Florence's Pitti Palace and Paris's Louvre and a succession of new books, but when asked what he considers the greatest luxury in life, the grand old man replies, "Simplicity."

PREVIOUS PAGE: *A stream bisects Horst's property, creating a soothing woodland scene.* OPPOSITE: *This watercolor was created in homage to Horst and his dachshund, Maxie.* TOP: *The house resembles a Tunisian bungalow.* BOTTOM: *A Korean dogwood grows near the gate.* FOLLOWING PAGE: *Two marble chairs, made for Napoleon's Venetian palazzo, reside on a terrace overlooking the stream.*

Time and Privacy 145

OPPOSITE: *Horst P. Horst.* TOP: *Cool and colorful in the summer sun, the garden room was photographed by Horst in 1990.* BOTTOM: *Horst composed his* Still Life with Flowers and Bocklin *in 1959.*

Graceful Vistas

"It's a real weekend house," says Lee Link of her "knotty pine" bungalow atop a hill in Sharon, Connecticut. "It's perfect for New Yorkers who don't need to think of themselves as living in the country." Lee and her husband, Fritz, maintain a proper Central Park West apartment during the week with attendant activities—he's an attorney, she's president of a charity group for children—and the country house nestled among three gardens provides a desirable antidote—"not exactly bohemian, but much more relaxed." Designed by a local architect, Ilsa Reese, the house is a flowing, airy structure perfect for summer living.

The garden room began life as an open-air corridor off the master bedroom, which quickly became a holding bin for Lee's garden tools ("otherwise I'd have to schlepp that stuff to the garage"). A few years ago the Links expanded the space by three crucial feet, which made the hallway wide enough to become a room. Connecticut's notorious bugginess demands screens, but otherwise the room is completely open. (The storm windows that provide protection in winter are removed in late spring.) Still packed with Lee's tools, now artistically arranged in an old tin washtub, the garden room also serves as a reading retreat, a private sitting area when guests stay at the house, or, on summer nights, a place to dry off after soaking in the hot tub.

The view of rolling hills is oceanlike in its magnitude and, with gentle breezes waving leafy fronds, is conducive to leisurely lounging. Compounding the cruise-like effect, the sense of luxurious travel, are the chairs, two wood-frame recliners with cane seats that once adorned the deck of some forgotten ocean liner.

Assorted objects—weathered finials, a Victorian dollhouse, an enormous glazed vase—have the random quality of flotsam and jetsam, but the chairs, unearthed separately in Vermont, carry the mood of the room.

The garden room opens onto a vine-covered pergola and a grass terrace wedged between herb garden and perennial borders, planned and planted by Lee, who had to take the vagaries of her landscape into consideration. "It's so steep here," she notes, "a pot will roll down the hill." She's in the process of building stone walls and more terraces and eventually plans a water garden.

Her husband does not share this gardening enthusiasm, and Lee can trace her green thumb only to a distant aunt. "My mother was a real geranium type. Consequently, I have not one geranium." She reflects a moment. "I don't think my mother ever even got her hands dirty. But one of my great pleasures is doing the garden myself, spending the weekend getting filthy dirty. It's a nice departure from the rest of the week."

PREVIOUS PAGE: *Treasures such as weathered wooden finials, garden ornaments, and antique books were accumulated over time.* OPPOSITE: *The garden room is a screened porch that opens onto a grass terrace. Unexpected objects include a large glazed urn,* TOP, *and a Victorian dollhouse,* BOTTOM. FOLLOWING PAGE: *A daybed under the wisteria- and morning glory–laden pergola is a lovely place from which to enjoy the view.*

Time and Privacy 153

ABOVE: *Two steamer deck chairs give the garden room its sense of comfortable lounging. A collection of hoes, rakes, and edgers juts out of an old-fashioned tin washtub.* OPPOSITE: *Lee Link.*

Porch Classicism

"I'm just as amateurish as anybody," insists Gregory Long, president of the New York Botanical Garden. "I've been gardening since 1974, but I'm not a horticulturist. It's coincidence, in a way, that I hold this job." Gregory, who worked at the New York Public Library and the American Museum of Natural History before his current position, is unduly modest about his gardening achievements. He does stress, however, that he doesn't make use of the contacts the NYBG could easily provide him in creating his retreat—the Greek Revival house in Otego, New York, where he weekends is his arena alone, although he did call on his friend, garden designer Hitch Lyman, to fashion a sunken blue and white garden.

The "plain old white-clapboard house" built in 1835, which Gregory bought for a song in the early 1970s, is an idyllic refuge set in the middle of a dairy farming valley and surrounded by a 400-acre view of meadows, woods, blue mountains, and a young apple and pear orchard stretching up the hillside. Gregory came to gardening through architecture, and the intersecting history of the two fields has provided a constant "avocational interest" for him. Challenged by the notion of making a garden stylistically and historically appropriate to the house, he has created one brilliant in its simplicity. The walls of the white clapboard house and the green hemlock hedges frame areas planted as much as possible with the native species available to his early-nineteenth-century predecessors, though Gregory readily acknowledges that his vision reveals influences, such as Vita Sackville-West's garden at Sissinghurst or the "stone-floored terraces of Pompeii," unknown to them.

A small study upstairs holds Gregory's library, an extensive collection of books on gardens, architecture, and travel. One of his great interests is "the Grand Tour" undertaken by eighteenth- and nineteenth-century Britons and Americans, and the effect of Italian taste on buildings and gardens back home. The study also houses the notebooks Gregory has been keeping for years, unassuming spiral-bound journals that record trips, ideas, and the weekly vicissitudes of his garden.

"I'm lucky because there's an excellent climate here for gardening," he explains, "very cold at night and warm during the days." The short season means that the cosmos, garden phlox, asters, and sedum 'Autumn Joy' of the pink, red, and white garden are ablaze during August and September, even if early frosts temporarily nip their enthusiasm. At the back of the house a stone terrace carved out from the hillside has been planted with lichens, mosses, and creeping herbs such as thyme, and it connects the house to the pink garden.

One of the most beautiful elements of all is the porch, Gregory's favorite spot in the garden. Elegant and dignified now, the porch was actually a collapsing woodshed attached to the kitchen that Gregory restored and transformed into a mini temple, complete with a Doric front. Its paved floor leads directly into glass-paned doors in the kitchen and dining room, making the porch a wonderful place for meals. On sunny days the white walls and stone floor trap heat, making the area "hot and aromatic" with the scent of herbs: tarragon and sage grown in pots, and thyme in between the paving stones on the terrace. But best of

all, perhaps, are days when the weather is not so benevolent, and the landscape is wet and blurry. "I like to sit out on the porch in the rain a lot," Gregory says.

PREVIOUS PAGE: *In the late summer, a mass of pink phlox and cosmos borders the garden porch.* OPPOSITE: *One view from the porch is toward the orchard.*
TOP: *A scented geranium is the centerpiece of a table surrounded by simple painted chairs.* BOTTOM: *An orchard of apple trees was planted at the rear of the house.*
FOLLOWING PAGE: *Gregory Long,* TOP INSET, *writes in his garden journals every weekend.* BOTTOM INSET: *The Greek Revival house dates from 1835.*

Time and Privacy 161

...at its peak, although
...mmer is g...
...eins co... ...t raining...
...dges an... ...at this point by Ed...
...t They ...d in their new g...
...that m... ...me #is not very co...
...scrappy... ...good still. Will it
...record wor... ...ght? Maybe not.

August 2, 1992. Sunday Evening. 7 pm Has.
to leave for drive to N.Y.C.
Sunny, breezy, warm August da
A bit hazy + blue on the hills.
Weeding +
Feeling.
all is g
Bloom...

Relaxed Grandeur

When Renny Reynolds was eight, his next-door neighbor in Saint Louis, Missouri, showed him how to propagate pachysandra—"the neatest thing I'd ever seen." Several decades later, Renny's enthusiasm for nature, and its nurture, continues undiminished, though now he tends to orchids and designs exquisite floral extravaganzas in his Manhattan shop. As one of New York's foremost party planners and the author of a monthly magazine column on entertaining tips, Renny brims with good ideas and joie de vivre. This sense of friendly exuberance is even more pronounced in the seventy-two rolling acres of his Bucks County estate in Pennsylvania. It can be seen not only in the scale of the setting, which has all been "transformed into one sort of garden or another," but also in the bountiful vistas, ample plantings, and numerous structures, from barn, tool, and potting sheds (Renny is also opening up a sizable perennial-nursery venture) to apiary, fowl hutch, and pagoda. Renny is not one to scrimp and minge, whether it's in table decoration or in plants. (The first year after he bought the property, he planted 8,000 daffodils, which have all naturalized prolifically. He also cultivates 3,000 peonies in shades of white, pale pink, and burgundy.)

Renny's sense of scale indicates not so much an inflation of ego as a generosity of spirit. He shares the land with cows, horses, "a special line of sheep," Australian black swans (who have their own pool), turkeys, ducks, chickens, and a pack of dogs and cats, most of whom are ASPCA "pals." Renny's personality plus the demands of his highly successful business mean that Bucks County is at its best as a place for rest and rejuvenation. The design of the eighteenth-century

Pennsylvania

house, "as untouched as possible by the nineteenth and twentieth centuries," corresponds to the plainness of the barns and outbuildings, and the feel of this sprawling estate is one of luxurious simplicity. For all the property's grandeur, the atmosphere at Renny's is relaxed, with animals lolling about and a certain indifference to weeds and other potential gardening bugaboos.

Renny has garden rooms, both indoors and out, in a number of places. There's a thirty-foot-high pagoda-shaped pavilion set on the pond; a formal, box-decorated vegetable garden next to the chicken coop; and another white-fenced vegetable garden surrounding a birdbath, a quarter of which is devoted to flowers for cutting. But one of the most pleasant rooms is situated in the barn. Dust motes spin in the shafts of sunlight and cats doze on ancient tables and benches or on an old army kit bed. Straw and tools mingle with the odd museum of Renny's party props—wire baskets, antique urns, candelabra, glass vases, and fabrics—stored here until they can be of service. Though Renny is familiar with the highest of high society—he's designed White House party tables for the Nixons, Fords, and Reagans, after all—he might well be more at home in the lackadaisical disarray of the fragrant barn. It's the kind of place that reminds one of a certain type of Wordsworthian summer afternoon: "Sweet childish days that were as long/ As twenty days are now."

PREVIOUS PAGE: *The barn is one of several garden rooms.* OPPOSITE: *Watercolor impressions by Ivan capture the countryside around Renny's property.* TOP: *Renny planted an espalier fruit tree against the side of his barn.* CENTER: *A simple, painted black semi-circle changes the impression of the barn's door.* BOTTOM: *The toolshed has slatted walls for gardening implements.*

Time and Privacy 167

OPPOSITE, TOP LEFT: *This view of the garden shows the barn in the background.*
TOP RIGHT: *Candelabra decorate the lawn.* BOTTOM LEFT: *An enclosed garden looks down to the main house.* BOTTOM RIGHT: *Renny Reynolds by his pond and putti-encrusted fountain.* ABOVE: *Resident black swans swim in the reflection of the pagoda.* FOLLOWING PAGE: *Chez Renny.*

Time and Privacy 169

chez
Renny

Pennsylvania

TOP: *Cats enjoy the sun-filled garden room. A rooster and a spade,* ABOVE, *are part of life on the farm.* OPPOSITE: *Framed letters from Gertrude Jekyll to artist William Nicholson tell him she would rather be gardening during the day, but would sit for him at night. The result was her famous portrait, a postcard of which leans against that of another great gardener, Vita Sackville-West.*

172 The Garden Room

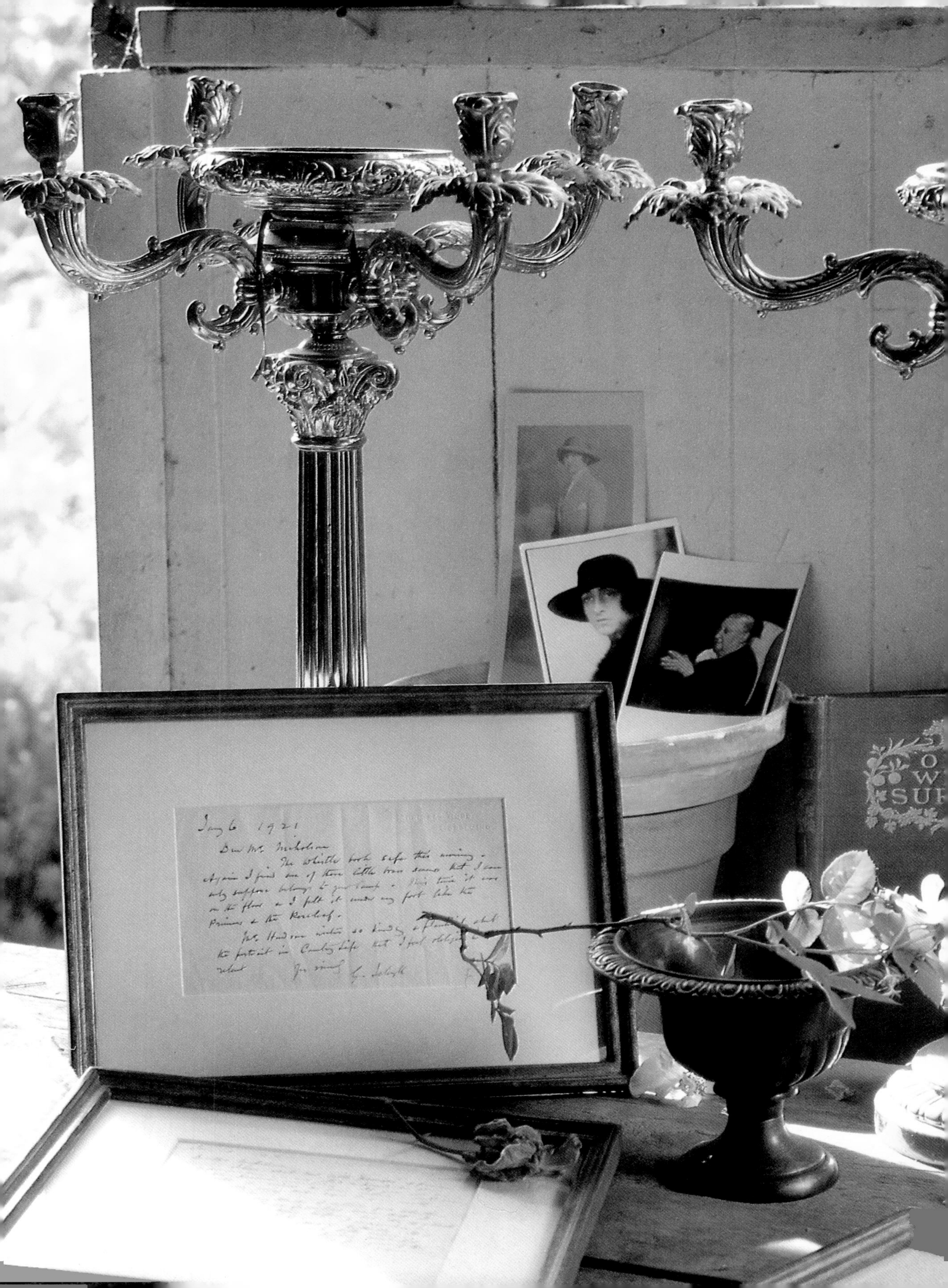

The Gardeners

Bill Blass is a widely acclaimed American fashion designer. He is the recipient of numerous honors, including the Coty American Fashion Critics Award, the *Gentleman's Quarterly* "Manstyle" Award, and, in 1987, the Lifetime Achievement Award from the Council of Fashion Designers of America.

Jutta Buck, a collector and dealer of botanical watercolors, prints, and books, has put together collections of botanical art and made appraisals. She lives in Stamfordville, New York, and is available by appointment.

Nancy Cardozo is the author of three volumes of poetry and a biography of Maud Gonne, now under contract to be made into a film by Angelica Houston. Her poems and short stories have been published in many magazines and quarterlies, including *The New Yorker, The Hudson Review,* and *Mademoiselle.*

David Easton's design firm has twice been awarded the Arthur Ross Award for architectural design for Georgian-style houses, and in 1992 he received *Interior Design* magazine's Hall of Fame Design Award. James Steinmeyer's interior watercolors have been featured in magazines such as *Town & Country, British House & Garden, HG,* and *W.* He has illustrated several books, including *Russian Furniture: The Golden Age* by Antoin Cheneviere and *A Passion for Detail* by Charlotte Moss. He won the Classical America, Arthur Ross Award for interior rendering.

J. Barry Ferguson is a renowned florist and lecturer; in 1988 the American Horticultural Society presented him with the Frances Jones Poetker Award for his contributions to the appreciation of creative floral designs. His book, *Living with Flowers,* received the first Design Committee Award from the National Arts Club and the "Quill and Trowel" Award from the Garden Writers Association of America.

Horst P. Horst's photographs have appeared in many publications. Recent books include *Horst: Sixty Years of Photography, Horst Interiors: 1950–1990,* and *Form,* as well as two forthcoming collections of travel and flower photographs. He has had retrospectives at the Palais du Louvre in Paris, co-curated by Richard Tardiff; the Ludwig Museum in Cologne; and the Pitti Palace in Florence. In 1993 he was honored with the Das Grosse Verienskreuz, Germany's highest decoration.

Robert Jackson, a decorative painter, has worked on many historic house restorations as well as with such decorators as Mario Buatto and Mark Hampton.

Ron Johnson is a landscape painter and has been designing gardens professionally for several years. George Schoellkopf, formerly a dealer in eighteenth-century American furniture and folk art, has written extensively on gardens and is a committee member of the Gertrude Jekyll Garden at The Glebe House in Woodbury, Connecticut, and the Garden Conservancy. He is presently designing a garden for his house in Santa Barbara, California.

Lee Link lives in New York, where she is active in many charitable organizations and currently serves as president of the board of Citizens Committee for Children, a New York advocacy group.

Pamela W. Logan is well known for her support of the arts in Boston and Ogunquit, Maine, where she lives and gardens.

Gregory Long was named president of the New York Botanical Garden in May, 1989. He previously served as vice president for Public Affairs and Development at the New York Public Library and created institutional development programs at the New York Zoological Society and the American Museum of Natural History.

Hitch Lyman is an artist and landscape designer. He has exhibited his watercolors in New York, San Francisco, Houston, and London. He has created gardens in Long Island, Connecticut, London, Spain, Italy, and Turkey.

Nancy McCabe has designed gardens for Kevin Bacon, William Paley, Mrs. John D. Rockefeller IV, Elyse Lufkin, and Bruce Kofner and Sarah Peter. Photographs of her gardens have appeared in many magazines.

Phyllis Meshover, a psychoanalyst, is an associate professor of psychology at CCNY, a supervising analyst at the William Aranson White Psychoanalytic Institute, and associate editor of *The Journal of Contemporary Analysis*. Michael Steiner's sculptures have been exhibited extensively throughout the United States and Europe and are owned by such museums as the Guggenheim in New York, the Hirshhorn in Washington, D.C., and the Museum of Fine Arts in Boston. He is a Guggenheim Fellow.

Renny Reynold's company, Design for Entertaining, has created parties for the White House, the Metropolitan Opera House, and the New York City Ballet. He has produced two videos on decorating and entertaining with flowers, is the author of *The Art of the Party*, and owns three flower shops in New York City.

Missy Stevens weaves rugs and creates miniature embroidered pictures; she shows her work regularly with Okun Gallery in Santa Fe and Mobilia in Cambridge, Massachusetts. Tommy Simpson makes wood sculptures and furniture and is represented by Leo Kaplan Modern in New York.

Jessica Tcherepnine has shown her botanical watercolors in London, Paris, and New York and has been in group exhibitions at the Hunt Institute of Botanical Documentation in Pittsburgh and other museums. She received First Place at the Greater New York Orchid Show in 1988 and two Gold Medals from the Royal Horticultural Society for a series of watercolors in 1988 and 1990.

Michael Trapp studied landscape design, art, and architecture at Ohio State University; his shop in West Cornwall, Connecticut, sells antiques and architectural fragments.

Bunny Williams, after working at the legendary Parish-Hadley decorating firm in New York for twenty-two years, started her own design company in 1988. With her friend John Rosselli, she opened Treillage in 1991, a shop on Manhattan's Upper East Side featuring unusual garden ornaments, antiques, flowerpots, and furniture.

Peter Wooster, whose company is called Mud & Mortar, has been an interior and architectural designer for the past twenty years. Recent projects have included several gardens and Orso, a restaurant with branches in New York, Los Angeles, London, and Toronto.

I N D E X